Web Security with Go

Build Safe and Resilient Applications

Tommy Clark

Discover other books in the series

"Go Programming for Beginners: Master Go from Scratch with Easy-to-Follow Steps"

"Web Applications with Go: Unlock the Power of Go for Real-World Web Server Development"

"System Programming with Go: Unlock the Power of System Calls, Networking, and Security with Practical Golang Projects"

"Go Programming for Microservices: Build Scalable, High-Performance Applications with Ease"

"Go Programming for Backend: The Developer's Blueprint for Efficiency and Performance"

"Network Automation with Go: Automate Network Operations and Build Scalable Applications with Go"

"Effective Debugging in Go: Master the Skills Every Go Developer"

Disclaimer

The information provided in *"**Web Security with Go: Build Safe and Resilient Applications**"* by Tommy Clark is intended solely for educational and informational purposes. While every effort has been made to ensure the accuracy and completeness of the content, the author and publisher make no guarantees regarding the results that may be achieved by following the instructions or techniques described in this book.

Readers are encouraged to seek appropriate professional guidance for specific issues or challenges they may encounter, particularly in commercial or critical environments.

Introduction

It is more crucial than ever to create safe online apps in the modern digital environment, when data breaches and cyberthreats are growing frighteningly frequent. Web Security with Go: Build Safe and Resilient Applications is your first step in learning how to create reliable, secure, and trustworthy applications, regardless of your level of programming experience.

Developers now consider Go (or Golang) to be a powerful language because of its ease of use, effectiveness, and scalability. However, the intricacy of protecting their apps from contemporary dangers might overwhelm even the most skilled developers when it comes to web security. This book fills that need.

Designed especially for Go developers, this article walks you through the fundamentals and best practices of web security step-by-step. The basics of protecting user data will be covered, along with how to strengthen your APIs and get practical experience with tools and methods that can shield your apps from threats like SQL injection and cross-site scripting (XSS).

When you can use Go's robust capabilities to create secure and high-performing applications, why rely on hunches or antiquated methods? You will have the skills and assurance necessary to foresee possible risks and design defenses that protect your systems and users by the end of this book.

Chapter 1: Web Security with Go Programming

In an increasingly digital world, web security has become a paramount concern for developers and organizations alike. As network breaches and data leaks proliferate, developers must be equipped with the knowledge and tools to build secure applications. This chapter focuses on web security using the Go programming language, commonly known as Golang, which is renowned for its simplicity, efficiency, and built-in support for concurrent programming.

1.1 Understanding Web Security

Web security involves protecting web applications from various threats, including attacks like cross-site scripting (XSS), SQL injection, cross-site request forgery (CSRF), and others. Each of these vulnerabilities can lead to unauthorized access, data breaches, or the corruption of data within web applications.

1.1.1 Common Types of Web Attacks

Cross-Site Scripting (XSS): An attacker injects malicious scripts into webpages viewed by users, potentially stealing cookies or session tokens.

SQL Injection: This occurs when an attacker manipulates a web application's SQL query by injecting malicious SQL code, allowing access to sensitive data.

Cross-Site Request Forgery (CSRF): A malicious site can trick a user's browser into making unwanted requests to another site where the user is authenticated.

Denial of Service (DoS): Attackers overwhelm and crash the application by flooding it with traffic.

Insecure Direct Object References (IDOR): An attacker accesses unauthorized data by manipulating input parameters.

Understanding these vulnerabilities is crucial, as they inform the secure coding practices that developers must adopt.

1.2 Why Choose Go for Web Security

Go has gained fame for its ease of use and performance. Its features make it an excellent choice for developing secure web applications:

Concurrency: Go's goroutines and channels allow developers to handle multiple tasks simultaneously, which can help manage security features efficiently, such as handling multiple authentication requests without blocking.

Simplicity and Clarity: The clean syntax of Go allows developers to write less complex code, which reduces the likelihood of introducing vulnerabilities due to misunderstandings or overlooked scenarios.

Strong Typing and Safety: Go's strong typing system

catches many errors at compile time, making it less likely that bugs due to incorrect data handling will make it to production.

Rich Standard Library: Go comes with an extensive standard library, offering packages for secure web server development, cryptography, and data handling, which are essential for building secure applications.

1.3 Setting Up a Secure Web Server

Before we delve into specific security practices, let's set up a basic web server in Go. This example serves as our foundation to explore various security measures:

```go
package main

import ( "fmt" "net/http"
)

func     HelloHandler(w     http.ResponseWriter,     r
*http.Request) {fmt.Fprintf(w, "Hello, secure world!")
}

func main() {
http.HandleFunc("/", HelloHandler) fmt.Println("Server
starting at :8080")
if err := http.ListenAndServe(":8080", nil); err != nil {
fmt.Println(err)
}
}
```

10

This simple application listens on port 8080. Our primary goal here is to build on this code, implementingsecurity features as we progress through this chapter.

1.4 Secure Configuration Practices ### 1.4.1 Use HTTPS

One of the most critical aspects of web security is ensuring all traffic is sent over HTTPS. This protects datain transit from eavesdroppers and man-in-the-middle attacks. Obtain an SSL certificate and set up your Go server to use it.

```go
http.ListenAndServeTLS(":443", "server.crt", "server.key", nil)
```

1.4.2 Set HTTP Security Headers

HTTP security headers help protect your application from certain classes of attacks. Commonly used headersinclude:

Content Security Policy (CSP): Helps mitigate XSS attacks by specifying which sources are trusted.

Strict-Transport-Security (HSTS): Enforces HTTPS connections for future requests.

X-Content-Type-Options: Prevents browsers from MIME-sniffing a response away from the declaredcontent type.

Adding these headers can be done using middleware in Go:

```go
func securityHeaders(next http.Handler) http.Handler {
    return http.HandlerFunc(func(w http.ResponseWriter, r *http.Request)    {    w.Header().Set("Content-Security-Policy", "default-src 'self'")
    w.Header().Set("Strict-Transport-Security",        "max-age=63072000; includeSubDomains")w.Header().Set("X-Content-Type-Options", "nosniff")
    next.ServeHTTP(w, r)
})
}

func main() {
http.Handle("/",
securityHeaders(http.HandlerFunc(HelloHandler)))
fmt.Println("Server        starting        at        :8080")
http.ListenAndServe(":8080", nil)
}
```

1.5 Input Validation and Sanitization

Proper input validation prevents many common web vulnerabilities, including XSS and SQL injection. In Go, it's vital to validate and sanitize all user inputs thoroughly.

1.5.1 Validating User Inputs

You might leverage libraries such as `validator` to ensure that user inputs conform to expected formats:

```go
import "github.com/go-playground/validator/v10"

type User struct {
Email string `validate:"required,email"`
}

func ValidateUser(user User) error { validate :=
validator.New()
return validate.Struct(user)
}
```

1.5.2 Escaping Output

When displaying user-provided content, escaping output
is necessary to prevent XSS:

```go
import "html"

func HelloHandler(w http.ResponseWriter, r
*http.Request) {userInput := r.FormValue("input")
safeOutput := html.EscapeString(userInput)
fmt.Fprintf(w, "Hello, %s!", safeOutput)
}
```

As we conclude this chapter, the importance of web
security in software development cannot be overstated. By
utilizing Go's rich features and adhering to best practices,
developers can build applications that are not only

functional but secure against prevalent threats.

In the following chapters, we will explore specific threats in greater detail, along with Go's libraries and techniques to safeguard our web applications further. By incorporating security at every step of the development process, you can significantly reduce vulnerabilities and protect both user and company data.

Installing Go and Setting Up Your Development Environment

Created by Google, it excels in building scalable, high-performance applications. Before diving into writing Go code, the first step is to install Go and set up your development environment. This chapter will guide you through the installation process and provide tips for creating an optimal environment for Go development.

1. Understanding Go

Before we jump into the installation steps, let's take a quick look at what makes Go unique. Go was designed with several goals in mind:

Simplicity: The syntax is clear and straightforward, making it easy to read and understand.
Concurrency: Go provides built-in support for concurrent programming, making it easier to write applications that can perform multiple tasks simultaneously.
Speed: Go compiles to native code, which means it

can run faster than interpreted languages. With these principles in mind, let's move on to installation.

2. Installing Go

Step 1: Check Your System Requirements

Before installing Go, ensure your system meets the necessary requirements:

Operating Systems: Windows, macOS, or any Linux distribution.
Architecture: x86-64 or ARM architectures.### Step 2: Downloading Go
Visit the official Go programming language website at golang.org.
Navigate to the Downloads section, where you can find the latest version of Go for your operating system.
Choose the appropriate installer for your system:
For Windows, you'll typically download a `.msi` installer.
For macOS, you will find a `.pkg` file.
For Linux, it often comes as a `.tar.gz` archive.### Step 3: Installation Process
On Windows

Run the downloaded `.msi` installer.
Follow the prompts to complete the installation. The installer sets up Go in the `C:\Go` directory by default.
Add Go to your system's PATH during installation (this is usually done automatically).#### On macOS
Double-click the `.pkg` file to start the installation.
Follow the installation instructions. By default, Go will be installed in `/usr/local/go`.
Ensure that the installation directory is added to your

PATH by adding the following line to your
`.bash_profile`, `.zshrc`, or equivalent file:

```bash
export PATH=$PATH:/usr/local/go/bin
```

On Linux

Extract the downloaded `.tar.gz` file to `/usr/local`:

```bash
sudo tar -C /usr/local -xzf go1.<version>.linux-amd64.tar.gz
```

Replace `<version>` with the version number of the Go package you downloaded.

Add Go to your PATH by modifying your profile file (e.g., `.bash_profile` or `.bashrc`):

```bash
export PATH=$PATH:/usr/local/go/bin
```

Reload your shell configuration:

```bash
source ~/.bash_profile
```

Step 4: Verify the Installation

Once Go is installed, verify that the installation was successful by opening a terminal or command prompt and typing:

```bash
go version
```

You should see the installed version of Go displayed. If you get an error message, double-check the PATH settings.

3. Configuring Your Workspace

Go uses a unique workspace structure, emphasizing organization and modularity. By default, Go projects are managed in a workspace that contains three directories: `src`, `pkg`, and `bin`. Here's how to set up your Go workspace:

Step 1: Create Your Workspace

Create a directory to serve as your Go workspace. You can create it wherever you prefer, but a common convention is to place it within your home directory:

```bash
mkdir -p ~/go/{src,pkg,bin}
```

Step 2: Set the GOPATH Environment Variable

Set the `GOPATH` environment variable to point to your

workspace. Depending on your operating system, add the following line to your profile file:

```bash
export GOPATH=$HOME/go
```

Step 3: Install a Go IDE or Editor

Having a good Integrated Development Environment (IDE) or text editor can significantly improve your productivity. Here are a few popular tools for Go development:

Visual Studio Code: A lightweight but powerful code editor that supports Go through the Go extension.
GoLand: A commercial IDE by JetBrains that offers advanced features for Go development.
Sublime Text: A versatile editor that can be tailored for Go development with the right packages.
Vim/Neovim: Highly customizable editors favored by many developers for their efficiency. ### Step 4: Install Go Tools
For improved development experience, consider installing additional Go tools. You can use `go get` to install packages and tools. For instance, to install `golint`, use:

```bash
go get golang.org/x/lint/golint
```

4. Writing Your First Go Program

Now that you've installed Go and set up your development environment, it's time to write your first Go program.

Create a new directory within your `src` folder:

```bash
mkdir -p $GOPATH/src/hello
```

Inside the `hello` directory, create a file named `main.go`:

```go
package mainimport "fmt"
func main() { fmt.Println("Hello, World!")
}
```

To run your program, navigate to the directory and execute:

```bash
go run main.go
```

You should see "Hello, World!" printed on your terminal.

With Go now installed, you are ready to explore its powerful features and develop efficient applications. As you continue further into this book, you will dive deeper into Go's syntax, concurrency patterns, and librariesthat will enhance your programming journey. Enjoy coding in Go!

The Power Go for Web Security

This chapter delves into the significance of web security, exploring its foundational principles, the threats that necessitate its importance, and the measures that empower both individuals and organizations to safeguard their digital landscapes.

Understanding Web Security

At its core, web security refers to the safeguarding of websites and online services from various cyber threats. This encompasses a wide array of practices and technologies designed to protect online assets, ensuring that users can interact with websites and systems safely and confidently. The realm of web security encompasses not just the protection of hardware and software, but also the integrity of the data they hold, the privacy of users, and the overall functionality of online platforms.

The power of web security lies in its multifaceted approach. It integrates different techniques—ranging from encryption and secure coding practices to intrusion detection systems—to create a robust defense against a plethora of threats. To truly understand its power, we must first explore the myriad dangers that exist in the digital landscape.

The Landscape of Threats

The internet, while a remarkable tool for connectivity and

information, harbors numerous threats. Cybercriminals exploit vulnerabilities in systems, leading to data breaches, identity theft, ransomware attacks, and more. Common threats include:

Malware: Malicious software designed to disrupt, damage, or gain unauthorized access to systems. This can include viruses, worms, Trojans, and spyware.

Phishing: Deceptive attempts to obtain sensitive data, such as usernames or credit card information, often through misleading emails or fake websites.

DDoS Attacks: Distributed Denial of Service attacks overwhelm a target system or network with traffic, rendering it inoperable.

SQL Injection: A code injection technique that exploits vulnerabilities in a web application's software to access or manipulate database information.

Man-in-the-Middle Attacks: When an attacker intercepts and alters communication between two parties without their knowledge.

Understanding these threats underscores the crucial need for web security. The potential consequences of neglecting this need can be dire, not only resulting in financial loss but also eroding trust in organizations and their digital services.

Building a Strong Defense

The power of web security is most evident in the strategies and best practices used to build defenses against threats. It starts with recognizing that security is not a one-time effort but an ongoing commitment to protection and resilience.

Strong Authentication: Implementing multi-factor authentication (MFA) strengthens access controls, ensuring that even if a password is compromised, additional layers of security are in place to protect sensitive information.

Encryption: Encrypting data both in transit and at rest guarantees that sensitive information, such as personal data or financial records, remains secure from unauthorized access.

Regular Updates and Patching: Keeping software and systems updated is vital to closing vulnerabilities that cybercriminals might exploit. Regular patching can substantially reduce the risk of attacks.

Web Application Firewalls (WAF): A WAF acts as a shield between web applications and the Internet, filtering out malicious traffic and preventing attacks before they reach critical systems.

User Education: Empowering users with knowledge about potential threats, safe browsing practices, and recognizing phishing attempts enhances the overall security posture of any organization.

Incident Response Plan: Having a well-defined plan

in case of a security breach ensures quicker recovery and minimizes damage. This includes identifying roles and responsibilities in the event of a cyber incident.

The Role of Compliance

Compliance with industry standards and regulations enhances web security efforts. Frameworks such as PCI-DSS for payment data, GDPR for user privacy, and NIST cybersecurity standards provide guidelines for establishing secure practices and ensuring accountability. Organizations that prioritize compliance demonstrate their commitment to security, instilling confidence in their users and stakeholders.

The Future of Web Security

As technology continues to evolve, so too do the challenges and methods associated with web security. The rise of artificial intelligence and machine learning presents both opportunities and new vulnerabilities. While these technologies can be utilized for predictive analysis and threat detection, they can also be harnessed by cybercriminals to develop more sophisticated attacks.

Looking forward, the power of web security will increasingly rely on innovation and adaptability. As organizations embrace emerging technologies, they must remain vigilant, proactive, and flexible in their security strategies. Collaborative efforts across industries, sharing threat intelligence, and fostering a culture of security awareness are vital to building a more secure online environment.

The power of web security is not merely a technical requirement; it is a foundational pillar of trust in the digital age. As we navigate the complexities of the online world, understanding and implementing effective web security practices empowers us to protect our personal data, our organizations, and our collective digital future. By embracing a culture of security, we not only safeguard ourselves but also contribute to a safer, more resilient internet for all.

Chapter 2: Understanding Web Application Security Basics

Understanding the fundamentals of web application security is essential for developers, security professionals, and users alike. This chapter delves into the core principles, threats, and best practices in web application security, laying the groundwork for a deeper exploration of specific vulnerabilities in subsequentchapters.

2.1 What is Web Application Security?

Web application security refers to the measures and protocols put in place to protect web applications and their users from various security threats. Unlike traditional software security, which focuses on operating systems or network security, web application security addresses vulnerabilities that arise in the application layer. This includes various attack vectors such as malicious inputs, improper configurations, and inadequateauthentication mechanisms.

Key Objectives

Confidentiality: Ensuring that sensitive information is accessible only to authorized users.
Integrity: Protecting data from unauthorized modifications, ensuring that users can trust the information presented.
Availability: Ensuring that services are accessible and operational when needed. ## 2.2 Common Web Application Threats

Web applications face myriad threats that can compromise security. Understanding these threats is the firststep in developing effective security measures.

2.2.1 Cross-Site Scripting (XSS)

Cross-Site Scripting is a vulnerability that enables attackers to inject malicious scripts into webpages viewed by users. These scripts can capture sensitive information like session cookies, allowing attackers to impersonate users or steal data.

2.2.2 SQL Injection (SQLi)

SQL Injection occurs when an attacker can manipulate a web application's database queries by injecting harmful SQL code. If user inputs are not properly sanitized, an attacker can retrieve, modify, or even deletedata from the database.

2.2.3 Cross-Site Request Forgery (CSRF)

CSRF attacks exploit the trust that a web application has in a user's browser. By tricking a user into executing unwanted actions on a web application where they are authenticated, attackers can perform actionson behalf of the user, often leading to unauthorized transactions or data changes.

2.2.4 Insecure Direct Object References (IDOR)

Insecure Direct Object References occur when a web application exposes a reference to an internal object(like a file or database record) without proper authorization checks. Attackers can manipulate these references to access unauthorized data.

2.2.5 Security Misconfiguration

Security misconfiguration is one of the most common vulnerabilities. It can arise from default settings, incomplete setups, or overly permissive permissions. Attackers may exploit such misconfigurations to gain unauthorized access to the application or its data.

2.3 Best Practices for Web Application Security

To counter the threats to web applications, a combination of secure design principles and coding standards is essential.

2.3.1 Input Validation

Implement strict input validation to reject any suspicious or malformed data. Use whitelisting approaches (accepting only known safe inputs) rather than blacklisting (rejecting known threats).

2.3.2 Use of Prepared Statements

To mitigate SQL injection attacks, always use prepared statements and parameterized queries which separate SQL logic from data inputs, ensuring that user input is treated as data, not executable code.

2.3.3 Implement Proper Authentication and

Authorization

Establish robust authentication mechanisms, such as multi-factor authentication, to verify user identities. Additionally, implement strict authorization checks to restrict access to sensitive data and actions based on user roles and permissions.

2.3.4 Secure Session Management

Utilize secure session management practices, such as generating strong session identifiers, employing secure cookies, and implementing proper session timeouts. This minimizes the risk of session hijacking.

2.3.5 Regular Security Audits and Penetration Testing

Conduct regular security audits and penetration testing to identify and address vulnerabilities proactively. Utilize automated tools and manual assessments to ensure comprehensive coverage of potential security gaps.

In the following chapters, we will explore specific vulnerabilities and their mitigation techniques in greater depth, further equipping you with the knowledge necessary to build secure web applications. As the landscape of web application security continues to change, staying informed and vigilant about emerging threats will be imperative for any developer or security professional dedicated to safeguarding digital environments.

Common Web Vulnerabilities

They facilitate seamless interactions between users and services, enabling everything from e-commerce transactions to social networking. However, the very features that make web applications user-friendly also open the door to a myriad of security vulnerabilities. Understanding these common web vulnerabilities is essential for developers, security analysts, and organizations alike to safeguard sensitive data and maintain user trust.

1. SQL Injection (SQLi)

One of the most notorious vulnerabilities, SQL Injection occurs when an application improperly processes user input. By injecting malicious SQL statements into a query, attackers can manipulate databases, potentially gaining unauthorized access to sensitive information.

For instance, if an application accepts a username and constructs a SQL query without proper sanitization, an attacker might enter a username like:

```sql
' OR '1'='1
```

This alteration can bypass authentication mechanisms and expose all records within a database. To mitigate this vulnerability, developers should use prepared statements and parameterized queries, ensuring that user inputs are correctly escaped and cannot alter the SQL command structure.

2. Cross-Site Scripting (XSS)

Cross-Site Scripting vulnerabilities allow attackers to inject malicious scripts into web pages viewed by other users. When unsuspecting users load the compromised page, the script executes within their browser's context, giving attackers the ability to steal cookies, hijack sessions, or redirect users to malicious sites.

XSS comes in three forms:

Stored XSS: The malicious script is stored on the server (e.g., in a database) and served to users who request the infected page.

Reflected XSS: The payload is reflected off a web server, usually via URL parameters. The user has to click a specially crafted link for the script to run.

DOM-based XSS: The vulnerability arises from client-side scripts modifying the DOM, permitting attackers to execute scripts in the user's browser.

Developers can defend against XSS by validating and encoding user inputs, implementing Content Security Policy (CSP), and sanitizing output when rendering user-generated content.

3. Cross-Site Request Forgery (CSRF)

CSRF exploits the trust that a web application has in the

user's browser. An attacker tricks a victim into unintentionally submitting an authenticated request, potentially changing user settings, or performing transactions without their consent.

A common mitigation technique is the use of anti-CSRF tokens, which are unique and unpredictable values that are tied to user sessions. When a user submits a form, the application checks for the presence of this token. If it is absent or invalid, the request is rejected.

4. Security Misconfiguration

Security misconfiguration is a broad vulnerability stemming from default settings, inadequate server configurations, or lacking proper security controls. It can manifest in numerous ways, such as excessive privileges for users, open cloud storage, or unprotected directories.

To combat misconfiguration issues, organizations should adopt a security baseline—consistent measures to harden configurations across all environments. This includes regular audits, continuous monitoring, and utilizing automated tools to identify potential weaknesses.

5. Sensitive Data Exposure

Sensitive data exposure occurs when applications do not adequately protect sensitive data, such as passwords, credit card information, or personal identifiers. Many applications store or transmit data in an unencrypted format, making it vulnerable to interception through various means.

To safeguard sensitive data, developers should implement encryption for data at rest and in transit, enforce strong password policies, and ensure compliance with regulations like GDPR or PCI DSS that mandate data protection practices.

6. Insecure Deserialization

Insecure deserialization vulnerabilities occur when an application deserializes data from untrusted sources without proper validation. This can lead to remote code execution, authentication bypass, and data manipulation.

To mitigate this risk, applications should avoid deserialization of objects from untrusted sources and implement integrity checks to ensure that the data being deserialized is free from tampering.

7. Using Components with Known Vulnerabilities

Web applications often depend on third-party libraries and components. If these components are outdated or contain known vulnerabilities, they pose a significant security risk. Attackers often leverage these vulnerabilities to gain unauthorized access or execute targeted attacks.

To mitigate the risks associated with using third-party libraries, organizations should maintain an inventory of software components and dependencies, regularly update them, and monitor vulnerability databases for security advisories.

Understanding and addressing common web vulnerabilities are critical steps in building secure web applications. Security should be an integrated part of the development lifecycle, with best practices woven into the fabric of coding, testing, and deployment.

Security Layers and the Role of Go

As applications become more integral to our lives, the necessity to ensure their resilience against potential threats has grown exponentially. This chapter delves into the concept of security layers—also known as defense in depth—and explores how the Go programming language, with its unique features and paradigms, plays a vital role in implementing these layers effectively.

Understanding Security Layers

Security layers consist of multiple levels of safeguards put in place to protect an application against various types of security vulnerabilities and attacks. This multilayered approach ensures that if one layer is compromised, others remain intact, providing a robust defense mechanism. The security layers can be broadly categorized as follows:

Physical Security: Involves protecting the infrastructure where systems are housed, including servers, data centers, and network devices.

Network Security: Encompasses the measures that protect the network from intrusions and threats, including firewalls, intrusion detection systems (IDS), and encryption protocols.

Application Security: Focuses on securing applications by applying security principles during their design, development, and deployment lifecycle. It includes practices like code reviews, static code analysis, and employing secure coding practices.

Data Security: Ensures that data is protected throughout its lifecycle, including encryption, access controls, and regular data backups.

End-User Education: A critical layer often overlooked; educating users about security best practices and how to recognize potential threats can mitigate risks significantly.

Incident Response: Planning and preparation for security breaches, including incident response teams, procedures, and recovery plans.

Each layer should work in tandem with others, creating a comprehensive shield against various attack vectors.

The Role of Go in Security Layers

Go, also known as Golang, has gained immense popularity due to its simplicity, efficiency, and performance. With a native support for concurrency, static typing, and ease of deployment, Go proves to be particularly effective in building secure applications. Below, we will discuss how Go contributes to each of the aforementioned security layers.

1. Application Security

Go's robust type system and compile-time checks significantly reduce the risk of certain vulnerabilities such as buffer overflows and type mismatches. The language's built-in features like goroutines and channels facilitate safe concurrent programming, helping prevent common multithreading vulnerabilities like race conditions.

In addition, Go encourages the use of the principle of least privilege. The language's well-defined packages allow developers to compartmentalize functionality. This organization helps enforce access controls and reduces the attack surface of the application.

2. Network Security

Go excels in network programming, making it a popular choice for developing secure applications. The `net/http` package provides out-of-the-box support for Secure Sockets Layer (SSL) and Transport Layer Security (TLS), which are essential for creating secure HTTP connections. Developers can leverage Go's extensive libraries for implementing robust authentication and authorization mechanisms, using industry- standard protocols like OAuth2 and OpenID Connect.

Additionally, Go's built-in support for asynchronous programming makes it an excellent choice for writing high-performance APIs and services that can handle multiple connections efficiently while maintaining security.

3. Data Security

Go's strong emphasis on immutability and clear resource management aids in securing sensitive data. By following best practices such as never hardcoding credentials in the source code and using environment variables or secure vaults, developers can safeguard application secrets.

Furthermore, Go supports various libraries for encryption and hashing, ensuring that sensitive data is properly encrypted both in transit and at rest. The standard library includes packages like `crypto/aes` for encryption and `crypto/rand` for generating secure random numbers, which are essential for cryptographic operations.

4. End-User Education

While the programming language itself cannot educate users, the clarity and simplicity of Go's syntax can help developers produce more readable and maintainable code. Well-structured code can lead to better documentation and understanding of security practices among the development team. Developers can focus on security features and best practices, fostering a culture where security is a priority throughout the software development lifecycle.

5. Incident Response

Go's compile-time error checking and extensive testing capabilities contribute to quicker identification of vulnerabilities. Tools such as `go vet` and `golint` can help catch potential issues early in the development process. This proactive approach allows teams to respond quickly to vulnerabilities, minimizing the impact of potential breaches.

Incorporating logging and monitoring within Go applications is straightforward, enabling the collection of crucial data that can be utilized for incident response and forensic analysis. Libraries like `logrus` or built-inlogging packages facilitate the creation of comprehensive logs that track system behavior and security events.

As software applications continue to permeate every aspect of our lives, the importance of layered security cannot be overstated. The Go programming language provides a compelling foundation for building secure applications across all security layers. From robust application security features to efficient handling of network operations, data security practices, and incident response mechanisms, Go empowers developers tocreate secure systems that can withstand the complexities of modern security threats.

Chapter 3: Secure Authentication in Go

Authentication is the process of verifying a user's identity before granting access to resources. In this chapter, we will delve into secure authentication practices in Go, a powerful programming language known for its simplicity and efficiency.

We will cover various authentication methods and explore libraries that can assist in implementing secure authentication in Go applications while ensuring best practices are adhered to. By the end of this chapter, you should have a solid understanding of how to implement secure authentication in your Go applications.

Understanding Authentication

Authentication is fundamentally about asserting identity. It can take several forms, including:

Password-Based Authentication: The most common method where a user provides a username and password.

Token-Based Authentication: Users receive a token upon successful authentication, which is then used in subsequent requests.

OAuth and OpenID Connect: Protocols allowing third-party services to authenticate users on behalf of an application.

Multi-Factor Authentication (MFA): This adds an additional layer of security by requiring two or more verification methods.

Importance of Secure Authentication

The multitude of data breaches and security threats in recent years highlights the importance of secure authentication practices. Poorly implemented authentication can lead to unauthorized access, data theft, or account compromises. A well-designed authentication system not only protects sensitive information but also builds user trust.

Building a Simple Authentication System in Go

We'll begin by crafting a basic password-based authentication system in Go. The process will include user registration, secure password storage, and user login.

Prerequisites

Ensure you have the following packages:

```bash
go get golang.org/x/crypto/bcrypt go get github.com/gorilla/mux
go get github.com/dgrijalva/jwt-go
```

User Registration

Storing Passwords Securely: Use the `bcrypt` package to hash passwords. Never store plaintext passwords in your database.

```go
import (
    "golang.org/x/crypto/bcrypt"
)

// HashPassword hashes the password using bcrypt func HashPassword(password string) (string, error) {
    hashedPassword, err := bcrypt.GenerateFromPassword([]byte(password), bcrypt.DefaultCost)return string(hashedPassword), err
}
```

User Registration Handler:

```go
type User struct { Username stringPassword string
}
var users = make(map[string]string) // Simulating a database func RegisterHandler(w http.ResponseWriter, r *http.Request) {
var user User
err := json.NewDecoder(r.Body).Decode(&user) if err != nil {
http.Error(w, "Invalid input", http.StatusBadRequest)
return
}

hashedPassword, err := HashPassword(user.Password)if err != nil {
http.Error(w, "Error hashing password", http.StatusInternalServerError)return
}
```

```go
// Store the hashed password users[user.Username] = hashedPassword

    w.WriteHeader(http.StatusCreated)
}
```

User Authentication

Password Verification:

```go
// CheckPassword verifies the provided password against the hashed password func CheckPassword(hashedPassword, password string) bool { err := bcrypt.CompareHashAndPassword([]byte(hashedPassword), []byte(password))
```

```go
return err == nil
}
```

Login Handler:

```go
func LoginHandler(w http.ResponseWriter, r *http.Request) {var user User
err := json.NewDecoder(r.Body).Decode(&user) if err !=
nil {
http.Error(w, "Invalid input", http.StatusBadRequest)
return
}

storedPassword, ok := users[user.Username]
if !ok || !CheckPassword(storedPassword, user.Password)
{http.Error(w, "Unauthorized", http.StatusUnauthorized)
return
}

// Generate JWT
tokenString, err := GenerateJWT(user.Username)if err !=
nil {
http.Error(w, "Could not create token",
http.StatusInternalServerError)return
}

w.Write([]byte(tokenString))
}
```

Generating JWT (JSON Web Tokens)

JSON Web Tokens are a compact, URL-safe means of representing claims to be transferred between two parties. To implement JWT in Go:

```go
var mySigningKey = []byte("secret")

// GenerateJWT returns a new token for a username func
GenerateJWT(username string) (string, error) {
token := jwt.NewWithClaims(jwt.SigningMethodHS256,
jwt.MapClaims{"username": username,
"exp": time.Now().Add(time.Hour * 72).Unix(),
})

tokenString, err := token.SignedString(mySigningKey)
return tokenString, err
}
```

Securing Routes with Middleware

To secure routes using JWT, create a middleware that checks for a valid token:

```go
func TokenAuthMiddleware(next http.Handler) http.Handler {
return http.HandlerFunc(func(w http.ResponseWriter, r *http.Request) { tokenString := r.Header.Get("Authorization")

if tokenString == "" {
http.Error(w, "Missing authorization header", http.StatusUnauthorized)return
}

token, err := jwt.Parse(tokenString, func(token *jwt.Token) (interface{}, error) {return mySigningKey, nil
})

if err != nil || !token.Valid {
http.Error(w, "Unauthorized", http.StatusUnauthorized)
return
}

next.ServeHTTP(w, r)
})
}
```

Best Practices for Secure Authentication

Use HTTPS: Always secure your application with SSL/TLS to encrypt data in transit.

44

Regularly Update Dependencies: Keep dependencies updated, and watch for security vulnerabilities.

Implement Rate Limiting: Protect against brute-force attacks by limiting login attempts.

Use Environment Variables for Secrets: Never hard-code secrets or keys in your source code.

Validate Input: Always validate user inputs to avoid common vulnerabilities such as SQL Injection and XSS.

Regularly Monitor and Audit Logs: Monitor authentication attempts and set up alerts for suspicious activities.

Implementing Secure User Authentication in Go

With increasing threats and data breaches, applications must enforce robust authentication practices. This chapter will delve into the principles of secure user authentication and provide a step-by-step guide to implementing these principles in Go (Golang), a powerful language known for its simplicity and efficiency.

Understanding the Basics of Authentication

Authentication is the process of verifying the identity of a user before granting access to resources. It typically involves three key components:

Identification: The user presents their credentials,

usually in the form of a username and password.
Authentication: The system checks the provided credentials against a stored set of credentials to verify identity.
Authorization: Once authenticated, the user is granted access to specific resources based on their permissions.

Threats to Authentication

Before implementing secure authentication, it is crucial to understand the common threats:
Password Attacks: Such as brute-force attacks, where attackers try numerous combinations to guess a password.
Phishing: Attacks that deceive users into revealing their credentials through fraudulent means.
Session Hijacking: When an attacker takes over a user's session, gaining unauthorized access. ## Prerequisites for Secure Authentication
Strong Password Policies: Users should be encouraged to create complex passwords.
Hashing Passwords: Store passwords securely using cryptographic hashing, making it difficult for attackers to retrieve actual passwords.
Use of Salts: Adding a unique salt for each password increases security by making precomputed attacks (e.g., rainbow tables) less effective.
Multi-Factor Authentication: Implementing additional verification methods can provide an added layer of security.

Setting Up Your Go Environment

Before we dive into authentication mechanisms, ensure that you have Go installed on your machine. Install the latest version from the [official Go website](https://golang.org/dl/).

Create a new directory for your project and initialize a Go module:

```bash
mkdir go-authentication-appcd go-authentication-app
go mod init go-authentication-app
```

Using Third-Party Libraries

While we can implement authentication from scratch, leveraging established libraries can save time and increase security. We'll utilize the following libraries:

Gorilla Mux: For routing requests.
bcrypt: For password hashing.
JWT-Go: For handling JSON Web Tokens for secure sessions.Install these packages using:
```bash
go get -u github.com/gorilla/mux
go get -u golang.org/x/crypto/bcrypt go get -u github.com/dgrijalva/jwt-go
```

Implementing User Registration

Start by creating a `User` struct to represent our user model. Also, create handlers to register new users.

```go
package main

import ( "fmt" "net/http"
"github.com/gorilla/mux" "golang.org/x/crypto/bcrypt"
)

type User struct {
Username string `json:"username"` Password string
`json:"password"`
}

var users = make(map[string]string) // A simple in-
memory store

// RegisterHandler handles user registration
func RegisterHandler(w http.ResponseWriter, r
*http.Request) {var user User
err := json.NewDecoder(r.Body).Decode(&user) if err !=
nil || len(user.Password) < 8 {
http.Error(w, "Invalid input", http.StatusBadRequest)
return
}

hashedPassword, err :=
bcrypt.GenerateFromPassword([]byte(user.Password),
bcrypt.DefaultCost)if err != nil {
http.Error(w, "Error hashing password",
http.StatusInternalServerError)return
}

// Store the new user (in production, use a database)
```

```go
users[user.Username] = string(hashedPassword)
fmt.Fprintf(w, "User %s registered successfully!",
user.Username)

}
```
`` `

Implementing User Login

Next, we need to authenticate users by verifying their
passwords.

```go
// LoginHandler handles user login
func LoginHandler(w http.ResponseWriter, r
*http.Request) {var user User
err := json.NewDecoder(r.Body).Decode(&user) if err !=
nil {
http.Error(w, "Invalid input", http.StatusBadRequest)
return
}

hashedPassword, ok := users[user.Username]
if !ok ||
bcrypt.CompareHashAndPassword([]byte(hashedPasswor
d), []byte(user.Password)) != nil { http.Error(w, "Invalid
username or password", http.StatusUnauthorized)
return
}

// Generate JWT token
tokenString, err := GenerateJWT(user.Username)if err !=
nil {
```

```go
	http.Error(w, "Could not generate token", http.StatusInternalServerError)return
}

	w.Header().Set("Authorization", "Bearer "+tokenString)
	fmt.Fprintf(w, "Logged in as %s", user.Username)
}

// GenerateJWT generates a JWT token for the authenticated user func GenerateJWT(username string) (string, error) {
// Token creation logic
}
```

Securing Endpoints with JWT

To secure routes, let's implement a middleware that checks for a valid JWT token before granting access to protected resources.

Generating and Validating JWT

Inside the `GenerateJWT` function, we can create a new token using the JWT library.

```go
func GenerateJWT(username string) (string, error) {
claims := jwt.MapClaims{
"username": username,
"exp": time.Now().Add(time.Hour * 1).Unix(),
```

```go
}
token := jwt.NewWithClaims(jwt.SigningMethodHS256,
claims)                                      return
token.SignedString([]byte("your_secret_key"))
}

// Middleware for verifying JWT
func          VerifyJWT(next          http.HandlerFunc)
http.HandlerFunc {
return http.HandlerFunc(func(w http.ResponseWriter, r
*http.Request)         {         tokenString         :=
r.Header.Get("Authorization")
if tokenString == "" {
http.Error(w,   "Authorization   token   is   missing",
http.StatusUnauthorized)return
}
tokenString = strings.TrimPrefix(tokenString, "Bearer ")

claims := &jwt.MapClaims{}
token, err := jwt.ParseWithClaims(tokenString, claims,
func(token *jwt.Token) (interface{}, error) { return
[]byte("your_secret_key"), nil
})

if err != nil || !token.Valid {
http.Error(w, "Invalid token", http.StatusUnauthorized)
return
}

// Pass along the username from the token
r.Header.Set("Username",
(*claims)["username"].(string))next.ServeHTTP(w, r)
})
```

```
}
` ` `
```

We explored best practices for registration and login processes, as well as how to create and verify JSON Web Tokens. While this example provides a solid foundation, remember that secure authentication is an evolving field; staying updated with the latest security practices and having regular code reviews are crucial for maintaining security.

Session Management and Secure Tokens

Gone are the days when a simple username-password combination sufficed. Today, web applications must ensure that user sessions are secure and efficiently managed throughout their lifecycle. This chapter discusses how session management is implemented in Go, delving into the use of secure tokens for enhancing security.

Understanding Sessions

A session represents a temporary interaction between a user and a web application. It allows for a personalized experience, maintaining state across multiple requests. This might include keeping track of user preferences, authentication success, and user-specific data.

A session is typically established when a user logs in, and it is maintained until they log out or the session expires. In web development, session management can be achieved in several ways, including using cookies, server-side storage, or tokens.

Session Management Techniques ### Server-Side Sessions
Server-side sessions involve storing session data on the server. When a user logs in, their respective session data is stored, often in memory, databases, or file systems. A session ID is sent to the client, usually in the form of a cookie.

Advantages:
Centralized management of user sessions.
Ability to invalidate sessions easily from the server.

Disadvantages:
Requires server resources for storing session data.
Scaling can become a challenge as session data grows. ### Client-Side Sessions with Secure Tokens
An increasingly popular strategy is using secure tokens. Instead of storing session data on the server, you generate a token that contains all necessary details, which the client can then send back with each request. This token can be signed (and optionally encrypted) to verify its authenticity while preventing tampering.

JSON Web Tokens (JWT)

JSON Web Tokens (JWT) are a common format for secure tokens. A JWT consists of three parts:
Header: Contains metadata about how the token is generated, including the signing algorithm.
Payload: Contains the claims (information) that the

token conveys about the user, like user ID and roles.
Signature: Created by encoding the header and payload, then signing them with a secret key, ensuring that the token has not been altered.

Implementing Session Management with JWT in Go

The Go programming language provides rich libraries to handle JWT, making it straightforward to implement secure session management. Below is a simplified example of how to create and validate JWTs in a Go web application.

Setup

First, install the `github.com/dgrijalva/jwt-go` package using:

```bash
go get github.com/dgrijalva/jwt-go
```

Generating a JWT

```go
package main

import ( "fmt" "net/http""time"

jwt "github.com/dgrijalva/jwt-go"
)

var secretKey = []byte("your-secret-key")
```

```go
func generateJWT(username string) (string, error) {
claims := jwt.MapClaims{
"username": username,
"exp": time.Now().Add(time.Hour * 1).Unix(),
}

token := jwt.NewWithClaims(jwt.SigningMethodHS256,
claims)

return token.SignedString(secretKey)
}

func    loginHandler(w    http.ResponseWriter,    r
*http.Request) {username := r.FormValue("username")

// You should validate the username and password here
token, err := generateJWT(username)
if err != nil {
http.Error(w, err.Error(), http.StatusInternalServerError)
return
}

http.SetCookie(w, &http.Cookie{Name: "token",
Value: token,Path: "/",
HttpOnly: true, // Mitigates risk of client-side script
accessing the token
})

fmt.Fprintln(w, "Login successful, token created.")
}
```
```
```

The `generateJWT` function creates a token for the user that expires after one hour. The cookie is set to `HttpOnly` to mitigate XSS attacks by preventing client-side scripts from accessing the token. #### Validating a JWT
Next, validate the JWT in your authenticated endpoints:

```go
func validateJWT(w http.ResponseWriter, r *http.Request) {cookie, err := r.Cookie("token")
if err != nil {
http.Error(w, "Unauthorized", http.StatusUnauthorized)
return
}

tokenString := cookie.Valueclaims := jwt.MapClaims{}

token, err := jwt.ParseWithClaims(tokenString, claims, func(token *jwt.Token) (interface{}, error) { return secretKey, nil
})

if err != nil || !token.Valid {
http.Error(w, "Unauthorized", http.StatusUnauthorized)
return
}

fmt.Fprintf(w, "Welcome %s!", claims["username"])
}
```

This function retrieves the token from the cookie and validates it. If the token is invalid or expired, it returns an

`Unauthorized` error.

Security Best Practices

Secret management: Keep your secret keys secure and use environment variables to manage them.
Token expiration: Implement short-lived tokens and refresh tokens to reduce the impact of token theft.
Revoke tokens: Maintain a blacklist of revoked tokens if a user logs out or changes their password.
Use HTTPS: Always serve your application over HTTPS to protect against man-in-the-middle attacks.

Session management and secure tokens are essential components of modern web applications. Go's robust libraries simplify the task, enabling developers to securely manage user sessions with JWTs. By understanding and implementing best practices in session management, developers can protect user data while providing a seamless application experience. The combination of Go's efficient performance and secure session handling creates powerful opportunities for building reliable, scalable web applications.

Chapter 4: Encryption Fundamentals in Go

With sensitive data constantly being transmitted across networks, encryption plays a vital role in safeguarding information from unauthorized access. In this chapter, we will explore the fundamental concepts of encryption, focusing on how to implement these principles using the Go programming language.

4.1 Understanding Encryption

Encryption is the process of encoding information in such a way that only authorized parties can access it. This is achieved by transforming plain text into ciphertext, which appears incomprehensible to anyone who does not possess the decryption key. The primary goal of encryption is to protect confidentiality and ensure that data remains secure during transmission or while stored.

4.1.1 Types of Encryption

Encryption can be broadly categorized into two types: symmetric and asymmetric encryption.

Symmetric Encryption: This type uses the same key for both encryption and decryption. It is crucial that the key remains confidential, as anyone with access to the key can decrypt the information. Common symmetric encryption algorithms include AES (Advanced Encryption Standard), DES (Data Encryption Standard), and RC4.

Asymmetric Encryption: Also known as public-key encryption, this method utilizes two keys—one public and one private. The public key is distributed openly, while the private key is kept secret. Data encrypted with the public key can only be decrypted with the corresponding private key. This method ensures secure key exchange and is foundational for protocols like SSL/TLS. Common asymmetric algorithms include RSA (Rivest-Shamir-Adleman) and ECC (Elliptic Curve Cryptography).

4.1.2 Hash Functions

While strictly not encryption, hash functions are a crucial part of data integrity and security. A hash function transforms input data into a fixed-size string of characters, which is typically a hexadecimal representation. The output, known as a hash, is unique to each unique input, making it useful for verifying information integrity. Common hash algorithms include SHA (Secure Hash Algorithm) and MD5 (Message Digest Algorithm).

4.2 Implementing Encryption in Go

Go, also known as Golang, provides robust libraries for implementing encryption algorithms. The `crypto` package in Go's standard library offers functionalities for both symmetric and asymmetric encryption, as well as hashing. Let's explore how to use these libraries for basic encryption tasks.

4.2.1 Symmetric Encryption with AES

To perform symmetric encryption using AES in Go, follow these steps:

Import the Required Packages

```go
import (
"crypto/aes" "crypto/cipher""crypto/rand"

"encoding/hex""fmt"
"io"
)
```

Encrypting Data

```go
func encrypt(plainText string, key []byte) (string, error) {
block, err := aes.NewCipher(key)
if err != nil { return "", err
}

plainTextBytes := []byte(plainText)
// Ensure the plaintext length is a multiple of the block sizeplainTextBytes = pad(plainTextBytes, aes.BlockSize)

cipherText := make([]byte, aes.BlockSize+len(plainTextBytes))                iv := cipherText[:aes.BlockSize]

if _, err := io.ReadFull(rand.Reader, iv); err != nil {return "", err
}
```

```go
mode      :=      cipher.NewCBCEncrypter(block,      iv)
mode.CryptBlocks(cipherText[aes.BlockSize:],
plainTextBytes)

return hex.EncodeToString(cipherText), nil
}

func pad(src []byte, blockSize int) []byte { padding :=
blockSize - len(src)%blockSize
padText := bytes.Repeat([]byte{byte(padding)}, padding)
return append(src, padText...)
}
```
```

**Decrypting Data**

```go
func decrypt(cipherText string, key []byte) (string, error) {
cipherTextBytes, err := hex.DecodeString(cipherText)
if err != nil { return "", err
}

block, err := aes.NewCipher(key)if err != nil {
return "", err
}

if len(cipherTextBytes) < aes.BlockSize { return "",
fmt.Errorf("cipherText too short")
}

iv := cipherTextBytes[:aes.BlockSize] cipherTextBytes =
cipherTextBytes[aes.BlockSize:]
```
```

```go
mode := cipher.NewCBCDecrypter(block, iv)
mode.CryptBlocks(cipherTextBytes, cipherTextBytes)

// Remove padding
unpad := int(cipherTextBytes[len(cipherTextBytes)-1])
return string(cipherTextBytes[:len(cipherTextBytes)-unpad]), nil
}
```

Putting It All Together

```go
func main() {
key := []byte("examplekey12345") // 16 bytes for AES-128
plainText := "Hello, Golang Encryption!"

cipherText, err := encrypt(plainText, key)if err != nil {
fmt.Println("Error encrypting:", err)return
}

fmt.Println("Encrypted:", cipherText)

decryptedText, err := decrypt(cipherText, key)if err != nil {
fmt.Println("Error decrypting:", err)return
}

fmt.Println("Decrypted:", decryptedText)
}
```

4.2.2 Asymmetric Encryption with RSA

Asymmetric encryption is handled differently in Go. Let's create a simple implementation of RSA encryption and decryption:

Import the Necessary Packages

```go
import (
"crypto/rand"          "crypto/rsa"          "crypto/x509"
"encoding/pem"

"fmt"
)
```

Generating Keys

```go
func generateRSAKeys() (*rsa.PrivateKey, *rsa.PublicKey)
{privKey, err := rsa.GenerateKey(rand.Reader, 2048)
if err != nil { fmt.Println(err)return nil, nil
}

return privKey, &privKey.PublicKey
}
```

Encrypting Data

```go
func       encryptRSA(plainText       string,       publicKey
*rsa.PublicKey) ([]byte, error) {label := []byte("")
cipherText, err := rsa.EncryptOAEP(sha256.New(),
```

```go
    rand.Reader, publicKey, []byte(plainText),label,
)
return cipherText, err
}
```

Decrypting Data

```go
func     decryptRSA(cipherText     []byte,     privateKey
*rsa.PrivateKey) (string, error) {label := []byte("")
plainText, err := rsa.DecryptOAEP(sha256.New(),
rand.Reader,privateKey, cipherText, label,
)
return string(plainText), err
}
```

Putting It All Together

```go
func main() {

privKey, pubKey := generateRSAKeys() plainText :=
"Hello, Golang RSA Encryption!"

cipherText, err := encryptRSA(plainText, pubKey)if err !=
nil {
fmt.Println("Error encrypting:", err)return
}

fmt.Println("Encrypted RSA:", cipherText)
```

```
decryptedText, err := decryptRSA(cipherText, privKey) if
err != nil {
fmt.Println("Error decrypting:", err)return
}

fmt.Println("Decrypted RSA:", decryptedText)
}
```

4.3 Best Practices in Encryption

While implementing encryption, it's essential to keep the
following best practices in mind:

Use Strong Keys: Avoid using short or easily
guessable keys. Use recommended key sizes for stronger
encryption.

Iv Generation: Always generate a new initialization
vector (IV) for AES encryption to ensure that the same
plaintext produces different ciphertexts.

Secure Key Storage: Implement secure methods for
storing and managing encryption keys. Avoid hardcoding
keys in your source code.

Stay Updated: Encryption standards evolve
constantly. Always use contemporary and well-tested
libraries and frameworks.

Legal Considerations: Be aware of local laws
regarding the use of encryption technologies, as
regulations may vary.

As data security continues to be a primary concern in software development, mastering encryption fundamentals is critical for anyone looking to build secure applications. In the following chapters, we will delve deeper into specific encryption protocols and their implementations in Go, exploring new avenues for maintaining data integrity and security.

Implementing Data Encryption with Go's crypto Package

Encryption is a vital component of modern software development, ensuring the confidentiality, integrity, and authenticity of data. With increasing concerns about data privacy and security, developers must leverage reliable cryptographic tools to protect sensitive information. Go, with its robust standard library, offers a powerful `crypto` package that provides various cryptographic primitives for implementing data encryption. In this chapter, we will explore how to make use of Go's `crypto` package for data encryption, focusing on symmetric encryption using AES (Advanced Encryption Standard).

1. Understanding Symmetric Encryption
Symmetric encryption is a type of encryption where the same key is used for both encryption and decryption. This simplicity makes symmetric algorithms like AES popular for encrypting data in applications. However, securely managing the encryption keys is crucial, as exposing them compromises the entire encryption scheme.

Key Concepts:
Block Cipher: AES is a block cipher that operates on blocks of data (128 bits at a time).
Key Size: AES supports multiple key lengths, including 128, 192, and 256 bits.
Modes of Operation: AES can work in different modes (e.g., CBC, GCM), which define how to encrypt data larger than the block size.

2. Setting Up a Go Project
Before we start implementing encryption, let's create a simple Go project.

```bash
mkdir go-crypto-examplecd go-crypto-example
go mod init go-crypto-example
```

Make sure to add the necessary packages:

```bash
go get golang.org/x/crypto
```

3. Encrypting Data using AES
In this section, we will implement a function to encrypt data using AES in GCM (Galois/Counter Mode). GCM is an authenticated encryption mode that provides confidentiality and data integrity.

Code Implementation

Here's a complete example demonstrating how to encrypt

and decrypt a message using AES:

```go
package main

import (
"crypto/aes" "crypto/cipher"

"crypto/rand" "encoding/base64""fmt"
"io"
"log"
)

// Generate a new AES key
func generateKey() ([]byte, error) { key := make([]byte,
32) // AES-256
if _, err := io.ReadFull(rand.Reader, key); err != nil {
return nil, err
}
return key, nil
}

// Encrypt data using AES GCM
func encrypt(plaintext []byte, key []byte) (string, error) {
block, err := aes.NewCipher(key)
if err != nil { return "", err
}

gcm, err := cipher.NewGCM(block)if err != nil {
return "", err
}

nonce := make([]byte, gcm.NonceSize())
```

```go
	if _, err := io.ReadFull(rand.Reader, nonce); err != nil {
		return "", err
	}

	ciphertext := gcm.Seal(nonce, nonce, plaintext, nil)
	return base64.StdEncoding.EncodeToString(ciphertext),
nil
}

// Decrypt data using AES GCM
func decrypt(ciphertextB64 string, key []byte) ([]byte,
error)        {        ciphertext,        err        :=
base64.StdEncoding.DecodeString(ciphertextB64)if err !=
nil {
	return nil, err
}

block, err := aes.NewCipher(key)if err != nil {
	return nil, err
}

gcm, err := cipher.NewGCM(block)if err != nil {
	return nil, err
}

nonceSize   :=   gcm.NonceSize()   if  len(ciphertext)  <
nonceSize {
	return nil, fmt.Errorf("ciphertext too short")
}

nonce,     ciphertext     :=     ciphertext[:nonceSize],
ciphertext[nonceSize:]plain, err := gcm.Open(nil, nonce,
ciphertext, nil)
```

```go
if err != nil { return nil, err
}
return plain, nil
}

func main() {
key, err := generateKey()if err != nil {
log.Fatal(err)
}

message := []byte("Hello, World!") fmt.Printf("Original
Message: %s\n", message)

encrypted, err := encrypt(message, key)if err != nil {
log.Fatal(err)
}
fmt.Printf("Encrypted Message: %s\n", encrypted)

decrypted, err := decrypt(encrypted, key)if err != nil {
log.Fatal(err)

}
```
```

}
fmt.Printf("Decrypted Message: %s\n", decrypted)
```

Explanation of the Code

Key Generation: The `generateKey` function creates a 32-byte AES-256 key using the `crypto/rand` package.
Encryption: The `encrypt` function:
Initializes an AES block cipher.
Creates a GCM cipher mode.
Generates a nonce for the encryption.
Seals (encrypts) the plaintext and returns the ciphertext encoded in Base64.
Decryption: The `decrypt` function:
Decodes the Base64 ciphertext.
Extracts the nonce.
Opens (decrypts) the ciphertext back to plaintext.
Main Execution: The `main` function showcases the full process of generating a key, encrypting, and decrypting a message.

4. Best Practices for Encryption
When implementing encryption in real-world applications, consider the following best practices:
Key Management: Use secure key management practices. Don't hardcode keys in your source code; instead, use environment variables or dedicated secret management systems.
Nonce Management: Ensure nonces are unique for each encryption operation. Using a secure random number generator, as in our example, helps achieve this.
Regular Audits: Regularly audit cryptographic implementations to identify and mitigate vulnerabilities.
Stay Updated: Keep abreast of the latest developments in cryptography as vulnerabilities may arise

71

over time.

By understanding the basics of symmetric encryption and employing best practices, developers can effectively protect sensitive data in their applications. The power and simplicity of the `crypto` package make it an excellent choice for building secure applications in Go, reinforcing the importance of data security in a digital world.

Secure Data Transmission Using TLS/SSL in Go

The Transport Layer Security (TLS) and its predecessor, Secure Sockets Layer (SSL), serve as industry standards for encrypting data transmitted over networks. This chapter explores how to implement secure data transmission using TLS/SSL in Go, a statically typed, compiled language known for its simplicity and efficiency.

Understanding TLS/SSL### What is TLS/SSL?
TLS (Transport Layer Security) and SSL (Secure Sockets Layer) are protocols designed to ensure secure communication over computer networks. They provide encryption to prevent eavesdropping, authentication to verify server identities, and data integrity to ensure that data is not altered during transmission.

While SSL has been mostly deprecated due to known vulnerabilities, TLS is widely used in modern applications and is actively maintained. Understanding the basics of these protocols is essential for anyone involved in developing secure applications.

How TLS/SSL Works

When a client and server communicate over TLS/SSL, they follow a series of steps known as the handshake process:

Client Hello: The client sends a message to the server indicating supported cryptographic algorithms and other parameters.

Server Hello: The server responds with the chosen cryptographic algorithm and sends its digital certificate to authenticate itself.

Certificate Verification: The client validates the server's certificate against trusted Certificate Authorities (CAs).

Session Keys Generation: Both the client and the server generate session keys that will be used to encrypt the data.

Secure Connection: Once the handshake is complete, communication can occur securely using the established session keys.

This process ensures that both parties are who they claim to be and that their communications remain private.

Implementing TLS/SSL in Go

Go provides robust support for TLS through its

`crypto/tls` package, making it straightforward to implement secure communication in your applications. Below are the steps to create a simple TLS server and client.

Setting Up a TLS Server

To set up a TLS server in Go, you need a server certificate and a private key. You can generate self-signedcertificates using the `openssl` command:

```bash
openssl req -newkey rsa:2048 -nodes -keyout server.key -x509 -days 365 -out server.crt
```

This command will create a private key file (`server.key`) and a self-signed certificate file (`server.crt`).Next, create a simple TLS server:

```go
package main

import ( "crypto/tls""fmt"
"net"
)

func main() {
// Load the certificate
cert, err    :=    tls.LoadX509KeyPair("server.crt", "server.key")if err != nil {
fmt.Println("Error loading certificate:", err)return
}
```

```go
// Create a TLS config and set the Certificates
config := tls.Config{Certificates: []tls.Certificate{cert}}
config.Rand = nil // Use the default random source

// Create a listener
listener, err := tls.Listen("tcp", ":443", &config)if err != nil
{
fmt.Println("Error starting server:", err)return
}
defer listener.Close()
fmt.Println("Server is listening on port 443...")for {
conn, err := listener.Accept()
if err != nil {
fmt.Println("Error accepting connection:", err)continue
}
go handleConnection(conn)
}
}

func    handleConnection(conn    net.Conn)    {    defer
conn.Close()
fmt.Fprintf(conn, "Hello, secure world!\n")
}
```

Setting Up a TLS Client

Now that the server is running, let's implement a simple TLS client that connects to the server we justcreated.

```go
package main
```

```go
import ( "crypto/tls""fmt"
)

func main() {
// Configure the TLS settingsconfig := &tls.Config{
InsecureSkipVerify: true, // Ignore unverified certificate
warnings for demonstration
}

// Connect to the server
conn, err := tls.Dial("tcp", "localhost:443", config)if err !=
nil {
fmt.Println("Error connecting:", err)return
}
defer conn.Close()

// Read the responsevar buf [512]byte
n, err := conn.Read(buf[0:])if err != nil {
fmt.Println("Error reading from connection:", err)return
}

fmt.Println(string(buf[:n]))
}
```
```

### Running the Example

Start the TLS server by running the server code in one
terminal.
Run the client code in another terminal.

You should see the client receive a message from the
server indicating that a secure connection has been
```

established.

Best Practices for Using TLS/SSL in Go

Use Valid Certificates: Instead of self-signed certificates in production, acquire certificates from trusted Certificate Authorities (CAs).

Handle Errors Gracefully: Always check for errors when establishing connections, and handle them appropriately to prevent information leakage.

Use Strong Cipher Suites: Ensure your TLS configuration uses strong cipher suites and regularly update them according to best practices.

Enable Security Features: Set options like `MinVersion` and enforce secure versions of TLS (like TLS 1.2 or higher).

Monitor and Audit: Regularly monitor your secure connections and audit certificates to ensure they are up-to-date and correctly configured.

By understanding the handshake process, implementing a TLS server and client, and following best practices, developers can ensure that their applications communicate securely. As cyber threats continue to evolve, securing data transmission will remain a fundamental aspect of software development, making knowledge of TLS/SSL essential for every developer.

Chapter 5: Preventing Injection Attacks

In the world of web development, these attacks typically occur when an attacker is able to manipulate an application by providing untrusted input that is executed in a way that compromises the application's integrity. This chapter focuses on preventing injection attacks in applications developed with the Go programming language, commonly known as Go or Golang.

Understanding Injection Attacks

Injection attacks involve the insertion of malicious code into a program, allowing an attacker to manipulate the execution of applications. The most prevalent forms of injection attacks include:

SQL Injection: Attackers insert malicious SQL statements into input fields to manipulate databases.
Command Injection: Attackers execute arbitrary commands on the host operating system via the application.
Cross-site Scripting (XSS): Attackers inject malicious scripts into web pages viewed by other users.

Go developers must incorporate security best practices to mitigate these vulnerabilities and ensure their applications are robust against such threats.

Principles of Secure Coding in Go

To effectively prevent injection attacks in Go, developers should follow fundamental principles of secure coding.

Some important principles include:

1. Validate Input

Input validation is the critical first step in preventing injection attacks. Go provides various libraries to help with input validation, such as the `validator` package.

Type Checking: Ensure that input conforms to expected types.
Whitelisting: Only allow known good inputs rather than attempting to define or blacklist malicious inputs.

Example of Input Validation:
```go
package main

import ("fmt"
"github.com/go-playground/validator/v10"
)

type User struct {
Username    string    `validate:"required,alphanum"`
Password string `validate:"required,min=8"`
}

func validateInput(user User) error { validate := validator.New()
return validate.Struct(user)

func main() {
user := User{Username: "testUser123", Password: "myPassword123"}if err := validateInput(user); err != nil {
```

```go
        fmt.Println("Validation failed:", err)
    } else {
        fmt.Println("Validation succeeded!")
    }
}
```

2. Use Prepared Statements

When interacting with databases, always use prepared statements or parameterized queries. This practice helps separate SQL code from data and protects against SQL injection attacks.

Example of Prepared Statement:
```go
package main

import ( "database/sql""log"
_ "github.com/lib/pq"
)

func queryUser(db *sql.DB, username string) (*User, error) {
stmt, err := db.Prepare("SELECT id, username, password FROM users WHERE username = $1")if err != nil {
return nil, err
}
defer stmt.Close()

var user User
err    =    stmt.QueryRow(username).Scan(&user.ID, &user.Username, &user.Password)return &user, err
```

```
}
```

3. Escape User Input for Output

Preventing cross-site scripting (XSS) attacks requires the proper escaping of user-generated content before rendering it in HTML. The `html` package in Go provides `template.HTMLEscapeString` function, which can be used to escape special characters.

Example of Escaping Output:
```go
package main

import ( "html/template""net/http"
)

func handler(w http.ResponseWriter, r *http.Request) {
userInput := r.FormValue("input")
escapedInput := template.HTMLEscapeString(userInput)
w.Write([]byte("<html><body>" + escapedInput + "</body></html>"))
}

func main() { http.HandleFunc("/", handler)
log.Fatal(http.ListenAndServe(":8080", nil))
}
```

4. Secure Configuration Management

Properly securing configuration values, especially in

81

production, is crucial. This includes avoiding the exposure of sensitive data like database credentials and API keys. Use environment variables or secure vaults for configuration management.

5. Regular Updates and Dependency Management

Keeping your dependencies up to date is vital for security. Go modules simplify dependency management, making it easier to update libraries. Regularly check for vulnerabilities within your dependencies using toolslike `go mod tidy` and GitHub's Dependabot.

Testing for Injection Vulnerabilities

While prevention is essential, testing your application for injection vulnerabilities should not be overlooked. Incorporating automated security testing tools into your CI/CD pipeline can help identify weaknesses before they are exploited. Some popular tools include:

Burp Suite: For penetration testing and vulnerability scanning.
OWASP ZAP: A full-featured security scanner for web applications.

Preventing injection attacks in Go requires a comprehensive approach, encompassing careful input validation, secure coding practices, and ongoing vigilance. By adhering to the principles outlined in this chapter, you can help to ensure that your Go applications are resilient against injection attacks, safeguardingboth user data and application integrity. Always stay updated on the latest security practices and tools to constantly reinforce your defensive strategy against evolving threats.

Protecting Against SQL Injection with Go

This chapter aims to illustrate how Go (Golang), a powerful and modern programming language, offers strategies and practices to prevent SQL injection vulnerabilities while interacting with databases. From secure coding practices to using Go's built-in capabilities, we will explore how to safeguard applications against these threats.

Understanding SQL Injection

Before we dive into prevention techniques, it's essential to understand what SQL injection is and how it works. SQL injection typically targets applications that construct SQL queries by directly embedding user input. For instance, consider the following naive query construction:

```go
query := "SELECT * FROM users WHERE username = '" + username + "';"
```

In this code snippet, if a user inputs `admin' OR '1'='1`, the query becomes:

```sql
SELECT * FROM users WHERE username = 'admin' OR '1'='1';
```

This query would return all users instead of just the intended one, demonstrating how SQL injection can be exploited.

Best Practices to Prevent SQL Injection in Go ### 1. Use Prepared Statements

One of the most effective ways to protect against SQL injections is to use prepared statements. Go's database/sql package allows developers to use parameterized queries that ensure user inputs are treated asdata, not executable code.

Here's an example using a prepared statement:

```go
stmt, err := db.Prepare("SELECT * FROM users WHERE username = ?")if err != nil {
log.Fatal(err)
}
defer stmt.Close()

var user User
err  =  stmt.QueryRow(username).Scan(&user.ID, &user.Name)if err != nil {
log.Fatal(err)
}
```

In this example, the `username` is passed as a parameter, meaning the database engine treats it as a value rather than part of the SQL command.

2. Use ORM Libraries

Object Relational Mapping (ORM) libraries, such as GORM or ent, abstract database interactions and provide built-in protections against SQL injection. Utilizing an ORM can simplify code management while enhancing security.

For instance, using GORM looks like this:

```go
var user User
db.Where("username = ?", username).First(&user)
```

GORM automatically handles the parameterization of queries, effectively protecting against SQL injection. ### 3. Validate and Sanitize Input
While prepared statements and ORMs significantly reduce the risk of SQL injection, it's also crucial to validate and sanitize user inputs. Ensure that any input data adheres to expected formats, types, or ranges. Using regular expressions or built-in validation functions can help enforce these rules.

For example, if expecting a username to only contain alphanumeric characters:

```go
```

```
import "regexp"

func isValidUsername(username string) bool { re :=
regexp.MustCompile(`^[a-zA-Z0-9_]+$`)        return
re.MatchString(username)
}
```
```

Always check that input fields conform to defined rules before they are processed by your application. ### 4. Limit Database Permissions
Minimize potential damage from an SQL injection attack by limiting the database permissions assigned to your application. Design your database role with the principle of least privilege in mind. Your application should only have the necessary permissions to execute its required functions, thereby reducing the potential impact of a successful attack.

For example, if your application does not need the ability to delete records, avoid granting DELETEprivileges.

### 5. Regularly Update and Patch

Keep your database drivers, libraries, and dependencies up to date. Security vulnerabilities are often discovered over time, and updates may include important patches that address these vulnerabilities. Regularly update your Go environment and the libraries you are using to ensure you benefit from the latestsecurity enhancements.

### 6. Logging and Monitoring
```

Implement proper logging and monitoring to detect any unusual activities or anomalies in your application. By tracking SQL queries and their execution, you can identify patterns that might indicate a potential SQL injection attempt. For example, use a middleware to log every SQL query executed and any errors generated.

```go
func loggingMiddleware(next http.Handler) http.Handler {
return http.HandlerFunc(func(w http.ResponseWriter, r *http.Request) { log.Printf("Request: %s %s", r.Method, r.URL)
next.ServeHTTP(w, r)
})
}
```

Protecting against SQL injection is a vital aspect of web application security, and Go provides powerful mechanisms to ensure that your apps remain secure. By using prepared statements, leveraging ORM libraries, validating input, limiting database permissions, and maintaining up-to-date software, you can significantly mitigate the risk of SQL injection attacks.

Safeguarding Applications from Command Injection

These vulnerabilities allow an attacker to control an application's environment and execute arbitrary commands, often leading to unauthorized access, data exposure, or even complete system takeover. This chapter delves into the mechanisms of command injection, how it can occur in Go applications, and strategies for mitigating these risks.

Understanding Command Injection

Command injection occurs when an application incorporates unsanitized input into commands that are executed at the operating system level. Attackers can exploit this by providing specially crafted input that alters command execution. For instance, consider the following pseudo-code:

```go
package main

import ( "os/exec""log"
)

func executeCommand(userInput string) { cmd :=
exec.Command("echo", userInput) output, err :=
cmd.CombinedOutput()
if err != nil {
log.Println("Error executing command:", err)
} else {
log.Println("Command Output:", string(output))
}
}
```

In the example above, if the `userInput` were directly controlled by an attacker, they might provide input like `malicious; rm -rf /`, leading to disastrous consequences.

Recognizing Vulnerable Patterns

The first step in safeguarding against command injection attacks is recognizing vulnerable patterns within your code. Here are some common patterns that can lead to such vulnerabilities:

Dynamic Command Assembly: Constructing commands using user input without proper validation can lead to vulnerabilities.

Improper Input Handling: Directly interpolating user inputs into command strings without sanitization or escaping.

Using External Libraries: Some third-party libraries may not adequately sanitize inputs or perform necessary checks, leading to potential vulnerabilities.

Securing Your Go Applications

1. Avoid Executing System Commands

Whenever possible, avoid executing system commands altogether. Instead, leverage native library functions that provide the necessary functionality without the risks associated with command execution. For instance, if you need to work with files, use Go's built-in file handling libraries instead of shell commands.

2. Use `exec.Command` Safely

When you must use `exec.Command`, always pass

arguments as separate parameters rather than constructing a command string. This helps to mitigate injection risks. For example:

```go
func executeSafeCommand(userInput string) {
// Ensure that userInput is strictly controlled and validated
validInput := sanitizeInput(userInput) // ensure sanitization mechanisms are in place cmd := exec.Command("echo", validInput)
output, err := cmd.CombinedOutput()if err != nil {
log.Println("Error executing command:", err)
} else {
log.Println("Command Output:", string(output))
}
}
```

3. Parameter Validation and Sanitization

When accepting user input, always validate and sanitize it. Implement checkers that restrict input to validcharacters, or patterns expected for commands. Regular expressions can be useful here:

```go import (
"regexp"
)

func sanitizeInput(input string) string {
// Example of restricting input to alphanumeric charactersre := regexp.MustCompile(`[^a-zA-Z0-9-_]`)
```

```go
	return re.ReplaceAllString(input, "")
}
```

4. Proper Error Handling

Part of safeguarding your application involves handling errors effectively. Ensure that any command execution or system calls are wrapped in robust error handling logic. This helps in not exposing sensitiveinformation through error messages.

```go
output, err := cmd.CombinedOutput()if err != nil {
	log.Printf("command failed with error: %s", err)

	log.Println("Output was:", string(output))
}
```

5. Use of Operating System Features

For user management or system-related tasks, prefer using Go's native libraries, such as the `os` and `os/exec` packages. Whenever possible, leverage features and interfaces that minimize the need for system commands.

6. Security Tools and Static Analysis

Implement security tools and static analysis to identify potential vulnerabilities in your application code. Tools like `gosec` can scan your Go code and help detect command injection and other security issues.

7. Stay Informed

Finally, the security landscape is ever-evolving. Regularly update your knowledge through community forums, security advisories, and relevant documentation. Adhere to best practices in coding, conduct regular code reviews, and stay aware of the latest vulnerabilities to keep your applications secure.

By understanding the mechanisms and patterns that lead to such vulnerabilities, Go developers can implement measures to safeguard their applications effectively. Through careful coding practices, validation and sanitization of inputs, effective error handling, and the use of built-in libraries over system commands, developers can build resilient Go applications that stand firm against command injection attacks. Remember, a proactive approach to security is vital to maintaining the integrity of your software in an increasingly hostile environment.

Chapter 6: Securing APIs with Go

An API, or Application Programming Interface, serves as the gateway between applications, enabling them to communicate and share data. However, this open communication can become a potential vulnerability if not secured adequately. In this chapter, we will explore various strategies and best practices for securing APIs built with Go, a language known for its simplicity, performance, and strong concurrency support.

Understanding the Importance of API Security

APIs have become critical enablers for modern applications, powering everything from mobile apps to enterprise software solutions. As businesses rely on APIs for communications, data exchange, and integration with third-party services, ensuring that these interfaces are secure against unauthorized access, data breaches, and malicious attacks is paramount.

Common API Security Threats

Unauthorized Access: Attackers might attempt to exploit APIs to gain unauthorized access to sensitive data.
Data Breaches: APIs that mishandle user authentication and data transmissions can lead to significant data leaks.
DDoS Attacks: Attackers can overwhelm an API with excessive requests, hindering service availability.
Injection Attacks: Improper input validation can expose APIs to various injection attacks, including SQL injection and XML injection.

Understanding these threats is the first step towards building a robust API security framework. ## Best Practices for Securing APIs in Go
1. Authentication and Authorization

One of the foundational elements of API security is robust authentication and authorization mechanisms. InGo, you can implement various strategies, including:

OAuth 2.0: A widely used authorization framework that allows third-party applications to access user data without requiring password sharing.
JWT (JSON Web Tokens): A compact, URL-safe means of representing claims to be transferredbetween two parties. JWTs can be used to authenticate API requests efficiently.

Example Implementation:

```go
package main

import (
"fmt" "net/http"
"github.com/dgrijalva/jwt-go"
)

var mySigningKey = []byte("secret")

func CreateToken() (string, error) {
t := jwt.New(jwt.SigningMethodHS256) claims := t.Claims.(jwt.MapClaims) claims["foo"] = "bar"
```

```go
claims["exp"] = 15000

tokenString, err := t.SignedString(mySigningKey)if err !=
nil {
return "", err
}
return tokenString, nil
}

func ValidateToken(tokenString string) (jwt.MapClaims,
error) {
token, err := jwt.Parse(tokenString, func(token
*jwt.Token) (interface{}, error) {return mySigningKey, nil
})

if claims, ok := token.Claims.(jwt.MapClaims); ok &&
token.Valid {return claims, nil
} else {
return nil, err
}
}
```

2. Rate Limiting

To protect against DDoS attacks, implement rate limiting
on your APIs. This can help ensure that a singleuser or an
IP address does not overwhelm your API with requests.

Example Implementation:

Using third-party libraries like `go-rate-limiter` or
building a simple middleware to track request counts can

efficiently manage rate limiting in your API.

3. Input Validation and Sanitization

APIs often rely on user input, making input validation and sanitization crucial in preventing injection attacks. Always validate incoming data against expected formats and types.

Example Implementation:

```go
func ValidateInput(input string) error {if len(input) == 0
{
return fmt.Errorf("input cannot be empty")

}
```

}
// Further validation can go herereturn nil

4. Secure Data Transmission

Always use HTTPS to encrypt data in transit. This ensures that sensitive data is not intercepted by malicious actors. In Go, you can easily set up HTTPS by using the built-in `http.ListenAndServeTLS` function.

Example Implementation:

```go
```

```
func main() {
http.HandleFunc("/secure-api", secureHandler)
err   :=   http.ListenAndServeTLS(":443",   "server.crt",
"server.key", nil)if err != nil {
log.Fatal(err)
}
}
```
` ` `

5. Logging and Monitoring

Implementing logging and monitoring will help detect
unusual activities and respond to potential security
threats swiftly. A robust logging system can provide
insights into API usage patterns and flag anomalies that
may suggest abuse or unauthorized access attempts.

6. Regular Security Audits

Even with the best practices implemented, regular
security audits should be part of the API lifecycle. Security
threats evolve rapidly; hence, continuous testing, such as
penetration testing and vulnerabilityassessments, should
be part of your development workflow.

Securing APIs is an ongoing process that requires
vigilance, adaptability, and the application of best
practices throughout the development lifecycle. By
implementing the strategies outlined in this chapter,
developers can significantly enhance the security of their
APIs in Go, safeguarding their applications and users
against potential attacks.

Building and Securing RESTful APIs

These APIs enable seamless data exchange and integration, making them crucial for building scalable and efficient web services. The Go programming language, also known as Golang, has gained popularity among developers due to its simplicity, performance, and strong support for concurrent programming. In this chapter, we will explore how to build and secure RESTful APIs using Go, focusing on best practices, tools, and techniques to ensure robustness and security.

Setting Up Your Go Environment

Before diving into API development, it's essential to set up your Go environment. Begin by installing Go on your machine. You can find the latest version and installation instructions on the [official Go website](https://golang.org/dl/). Once Go is installed, you can verify the installation by running:

```bash
go version
```

Next, create a new directory for your project:

```bash
mkdir go-rest-apicd go-rest-api
```

Then, initialize a new Go module with:

```bash
go mod init go-rest-api
```

This command creates a `go.mod` file that manages dependencies for your project. ## Creating a Basic RESTful API
To demonstrate building a RESTful API, let's start with a simple example: a task management application. The first step is to define the data model. We'll create a `Task` struct representing each task.

```go
package main

import ( "encoding/json""net/http" "sync"
)

type Task struct {
ID      int      `json:"id"`

Title   string      `json:"title"`      Completed      bool `json:"completed"`
}

// In-memory storagevar (
tasks = []Task{}taskID = 1
mu      sync.Mutex
)
```

Implementing HTTP Handlers

99

Next, we'll implement the HTTP handlers for our API. We will create handlers to:

Create a new task (POST)
Retrieve all tasks (GET)
Retrieve a specific task (GET by ID)
Update an existing task (PUT)
Delete a task (DELETE) Here's how to set up the handlers:

```go
// CreateTask handles POST requests to create a new task
func CreateTask(w http.ResponseWriter, r *http.Request)
{
mu.Lock()
defer mu.Unlock()

var task Task
if err := json.NewDecoder(r.Body).Decode(&task); err !=
nil {http.Error(w, err.Error(), http.StatusBadRequest)
return
}

task.ID = taskIDtaskID++
tasks = append(tasks, task)

w.WriteHeader(http.StatusCreated)
json.NewEncoder(w).Encode(task)
}

// GetTasks handles GET requests to retrieve all tasks
func GetTasks(w http.ResponseWriter, r *http.Request) {
mu.Lock()
```

```go
defer mu.Unlock() json.NewEncoder(w).Encode(tasks)
}

// GetTask handles GET requests to retrieve a specific
task by ID func GetTask(w http.ResponseWriter, r
*http.Request) {
mu.Lock()

defer mu.Unlock()

id := r.URL.Query().Get("id")for _, task := range tasks {
if task.ID == id { json.NewEncoder(w).Encode(task)
return
}
}
http.NotFound(w, r)
}

// UpdateTask handles PUT requests to update an
existing task func UpdateTask(w http.ResponseWriter, r
*http.Request) {
mu.Lock()
defer mu.Unlock()

var updatedTask Task
if                      err                      :=
json.NewDecoder(r.Body).Decode(&updatedTask); err !=
nil {http.Error(w, err.Error(), http.StatusBadRequest)
return
}

for i, task := range tasks {
if task.ID == updatedTask.ID {tasks[i] = updatedTask
```

```go
json.NewEncoder(w).Encode(updatedTask)return
}
}
http.NotFound(w, r)
}

// DeleteTask handles DELETE requests to remove a task
func DeleteTask(w http.ResponseWriter, r *http.Request)
{
mu.Lock()
defer mu.Unlock()

id := r.URL.Query().Get("id")for i, task := range tasks {
if task.ID == id {
tasks       =       append(tasks[:i],       tasks[i+1:]...)
w.WriteHeader(http.StatusNoContent)return
}
}
http.NotFound(w, r)
}
```

Setting Up the Main Function

We will now set up the main function to define the routes
and start the HTTP server:

```go
func main() { http.HandleFunc("/tasks", GetTasks)
http.HandleFunc("/tasks/create",        CreateTask)
http.HandleFunc("/tasks/update",        UpdateTask)
http.HandleFunc("/tasks/delete",        DeleteTask)
http.ListenAndServe(":8080", nil)
```

102

```
}
```

Testing Your API

You can now test your API using a tool like Postman or CURL. Start your server:

```bash
go run main.go
```

To create a task, send a POST request to `http://localhost:8080/tasks/create` with a JSON body like:

```json
{"title": "Learn Go", "completed": false}
```

Securing Your API

While building an API is essential, ensuring its security is paramount. Here are several techniques to secure your RESTful API in Go.

1. Authentication

Implementing an authentication mechanism is critical. One common approach is to use JSON Web Tokens (JWT). To integrate JWT, you can use a library like github.com/dgrijalva/jwt-go.

Example of JWT Middleware

Create a middleware to check for a valid JWT token in requests:

```go
import (
"github.com/dgrijalva/jwt-go""net/http"
)

var jwtKey = []byte("your_secret_key")

func Authenticate(next http.HandlerFunc) http.HandlerFunc {
return http.HandlerFunc(func(w http.ResponseWriter, r *http.Request) { tokenStr := r.Header.Get("Authorization")
claims := &Claims{}
token, err := jwt.ParseWithClaims(tokenStr, claims, func(token *jwt.Token) (interface{}, error) { return jwtKey, nil
})

if err != nil || !token.Valid {
http.Error(w, "Unauthorized", http.StatusUnauthorized)
return
}
next.ServeHTTP(w, r)
})
}
```

2. Rate Limiting

Implementing rate limiting can protect your API from abuse and overload. You can use Go libraries like github.com/gin-contrib/limit for this purpose, or create a custom middleware to track API usage.

3. Input Validation and Sanitization

Always validate and sanitize incoming data to prevent common attacks such as SQL injection and cross-site scripting (XSS). Use libraries like [`go-playground/validator`](https://github.com/go-playground/validator) to enforce rules on incoming payloads.

```go
import (
"github.com/go-playground/validator"
)
var validate = validator.New()type Task struct {
ID      int    `json:"id"`
Title   string                      `json:"title" validate:"required,min=3,max=100"` Completed   bool `json:"completed"`
}

func CreateTask(w http.ResponseWriter, r *http.Request) {var task Task
if err := json.NewDecoder(r.Body).Decode(&task); err != nil {http.Error(w, "Invalid input", http.StatusBadRequest)
return
}
```

```go
if err := validate.Struct(task); err != nil {
http.Error(w, "Validation failed", http.StatusBadRequest)
return
}

//... (rest of CreateTask function)
}
```

4. CORS Management

Control which domains can access your API using Cross-Origin Resource Sharing (CORS). You can use a CORS middleware like `github.com/rs/cors`.

```go
import "github.com/rs/cors"

func main() {
c := cors.New(cors.Options{
AllowedOrigins:          []string{"http://example.com"},
AllowCredentials: true,
})

mux := http.NewServeMux() mux.HandleFunc("/tasks",
GetTasks)
// Add other handlers...

http.ListenAndServe(":8080", c.Handler(mux))
}
```

5. Logging and Monitoring

Implement logging for troubleshooting and monitoring API usage. Use Go's built-in logging library or third-party tools like `logrus`. Additionally, consider integrating monitoring solutions like Prometheus to track the performance and health of your API.

Building and securing RESTful APIs in Go can be straightforward yet robust if you follow best practices and utilize the right tools. Employing the strategies covered in this chapter—like JWT authentication, rate limiting, input validation, CORS management, and proper logging—will help ensure your API is not only functional but also secure against common vulnerabilities.

API Authentication and Rate Limiting Techniques

With the growing emphasis on data security, performance, and user experience, implementing effective authentication mechanisms and rate limiting techniques becomes imperative. In this chapter, we will explore various methods of API authentication, as well as techniques for managing API usage through rate limiting, all within the context of the Go programming language.

1. API Authentication: An Overview ### 1.1 What is API Authentication?
API authentication is the process of verifying the identity of a user or system making a request to an API. Proper authentication ensures that only authorized users can access a service, protecting sensitive data and resources from unauthorized access.

1.2 Types of API Authentication

There are several commonly used authentication methods in APIs:

Basic Authentication: A simple scheme where credentials are sent in the HTTP header. However, it is not secure unless the connection is encrypted (e.g., HTTPS).

OAuth2: A more complex and widely-used framework that allows third-party applications to obtain limited access to a user's resources without exposing their credentials. OAuth2 uses access tokens, which are granted after user consent.

API Keys: A straightforward method where unique keys are associated with each user or application. These keys are sent with the API request, allowing the server to identify and authenticate the requester.

JWT (JSON Web Tokens): A compact, self-contained way for securely transmitting information between parties as a JSON object. JWTs can be used for authentication and are signed, ensuring their integrity.

1.3 Implementing API Authentication in Go

Let's consider an example of implementing JWT-based authentication in a simple Go API. #### Step 1: Install Dependencies
We will use the `github.com/dgrijalva/jwt-go` library to handle JWTs.

```bash
go get github.com/dgrijalva/jwt-go
```

Step 2: Create a User Model and Generate a JWT

```go
package main

import ( "encoding/json"

"net/http""time"
"github.com/dgrijalva/jwt-go"
)

var jwtKey = []byte("my_secret_key")

type Credentials struct {
Username  string  `json:"username"` Password  string
`json:"password"`
}

type Claims struct {
Username string `json:"username"`jwt.StandardClaims
}

func login(w http.ResponseWriter, r *http.Request) { var
creds Credentials

// Parse the request body to get credentials
if err := json.NewDecoder(r.Body).Decode(&creds); err !=
nil {http.Error(w, err.Error(), http.StatusBadRequest)
```

```go
	return
	}

	// Validate credentials (dummy check for demonstration)
	if creds.Username != "admin" || creds.Password != "password" { http.Error(w, "Invalid credentials", http.StatusUnauthorized) return
	}

	// Create a new token
	expirationTime := time.Now().Add(5 * time.Minute)
	claims := &Claims{
	Username: creds.Username, StandardClaims: jwt.StandardClaims{
	ExpiresAt: expirationTime.Unix(),
	},
	}
	token := jwt.NewWithClaims(jwt.SigningMethodHS256, claims)

	tokenString, err := token.SignedString(jwtKey)if err != nil {
	http.Error(w, err.Error(), http.StatusInternalServerError)
	return
	}

	// Return the token to the client
	json.NewEncoder(w).Encode(map[string]string{"token": tokenString})
	}
```

1.4 Middleware for Token Validation

To protect our API endpoints, we need middleware to validate the JWT token.

```go
func validateToken(w http.ResponseWriter, r *http.Request) { tokenStr := r.Header.Get("Authorization")

claims := &Claims{}
token, err := jwt.ParseWithClaims(tokenStr, claims, func(token *jwt.Token) (interface{}, error) { return jwtKey, nil
})

if err != nil || !token.Valid {
http.Error(w, "Unauthorized", http.StatusUnauthorized)
return
}

// If valid, proceed to the next handlernext.ServeHTTP(w, r)
}
```

2. Rate Limiting: An Overview ### 2.1 What is Rate Limiting?
Rate limiting is a technique used to control the amount of incoming requests to an API within a specified timeframe. It helps prevent abuse, ensures fair usage, and maintains performance under high-load situations.

2.2 Common Rate Limiting Strategies

Fixed Window: Limits the number of requests in a fixed time interval (e.g., 100 requests per minute).

Sliding Window: Similar to fixed window, but the time interval moves with each incoming request,providing a rolling count of requests.

Token Bucket: Requests are allowed up to a certain limit, and excess requests are only permitted iftokens are available in a bucket.

Leaky Bucket: Requests are processed at a steady rate, allowing for burst traffic but ultimatelysmoothing out the flow.

2.3 Implementing Rate Limiting in Go

We can implement a simple rate limiting mechanism using the `golang.org/x/time/rate` package.#### Step 1: Install the Package
```bash
go get golang.org/x/time/rate
```

Step 2: Create a Rate Limiter Middleware

```go
package main

import ( "net/http"
"golang.org/x/time/rate""time"
)
```

```go
var limiter = rate.NewLimiter(1, 5) // Allow 1 request per
second with a burst of 5func rateLimitMiddleware(next
http.Handler) http.Handler {
return http.HandlerFunc(func(w http.ResponseWriter, r
*http.Request) {if !limiter.Allow() {
http.Error(w,        "Too        Many        Requests",
http.StatusTooManyRequests)return
}
next.ServeHTTP(w, r)
})
}
```

Step 3: Applying Middleware to Routes

Now that we have the rate limiting middleware, we can
apply it to our routes.

```go
func main() { http.HandleFunc("/login", login)
http.Handle("/protected",
rateLimitMiddleware(http.HandlerFunc(protectedEndpoi
nt)))http.ListenAndServe(":8000", nil)
}
```

In this chapter, we discussed the importance of API
authentication and explored various methods such as
Basic Auth, OAuth2, API Keys, and JWT. We
implemented a JWT authentication system in Go,
allowingusers to log in and receive secure tokens.

113

Chapter 7: Data Validation and Sanitization

With the rise of sophisticated cyber threats, the consequences of neglecting these fundamental principles canbe devastating, leading to data breaches, unauthorized access, and compromised user information. This chapter delves into the significance of data validation and sanitization, explores various techniques and best practices, and discusses real-world scenarios that illustrate the importance of these processes in web security.

Understanding Data Validation

Data validation is the process of ensuring that user input is correct, meaningful, and secure before it is processed by an application. The primary goal of validation is to prevent the entry of potentially harmful data into a system. In web applications, data validation typically involves checking input against predefined rules or formats to ensure that it meets specific criteria.

Types of Data Validation

Client-Side Validation: This type of validation is performed on the user's browser before data is sentto the server. It enhances user experience by providing immediate feedback but should notbe solely relied upon, as it can be bypassed by savvy users.

Server-Side Validation: This validation occurs on the

server after data has been submitted. It is essential for ensuring that all inputs are thoroughly checked, regardless of any client-side validation that may have been performed.

Whitelist vs. Blacklist Validation:
Whitelist Validation: Accepts only explicitly defined valid inputs. For instance, if a user is expected to enter an email address, the validation checks it against valid email formats.
Blacklist Validation: Attempts to identify and block known bad inputs. This approach is less secure because it relies on constantly updating the list of prohibited values, which may not cover all attack vectors.

Importance of Data Validation

The importance of data validation cannot be overstated. Inadequate validation can lead to several vulnerabilities, including:

SQL Injection: Attackers can manipulate SQL queries by injecting malicious inputs, potentially gaining unauthorized access to sensitive data.
Cross-Site Scripting (XSS): Unsanitized input can allow attackers to execute malicious scripts in the context of a user's browser, leading to data theft and session hijacking.
Buffer Overflow: This occurs when data exceeds the buffer's capacity, potentially allowing attackers to execute arbitrary code.

By implementing robust data validation measures,

organizations can reduce the surface area for these types of attacks.

The Role of Data Sanitization

While data validation ensures that only valid data is accepted, data sanitization focuses on transforming user input into a safe and secure format before storage or display. Sanitization is critical for reducing the risk of injection attacks and other vulnerabilities.

Data Sanitization Techniques

Encoding: Encoding user input helps maintain data integrity when displayed in different contexts. For instance, HTML encoding translates special characters into their corresponding HTML entities to prevent the browser from interpreting them as code.

Escaping: This involves adding escape characters to input data, particularly in SQL queries or codesnippets, to prevent execution. For example, in SQL, escaping strings helps prevent SQL injection attacks.

Stripping: This technique involves removing potentially harmful characters from input data. For example, removing script tags can mitigate the risk of XSS attacks.

Normalizing: Normalization transforms data into a standard format, making it consistent and easier to process. For example, converting all text input to lowercase before storing it in a database can help prevent duplication based on case sensitivity.

Implementing Data Validation and Sanitization

To implement effective data validation and sanitization practices, developers should follow several best practices:

Use Security Libraries: Leverage well-established libraries and frameworks that provide built-in validation and sanitization functions. This reduces the likelihood of errors and ensures adherence to best practices.

Regularly Update Input Validation Rules: As threats evolve, so should validation rules. Regularly review and update input validation to keep pace with new vulnerabilities.

Conduct Security Audits: Perform regular security audits and code reviews to identify potential weaknesses in data handling processes.

Educate Developers: Foster a culture of security awareness among developers by providing training on secure coding practices and the importance of data validation and sanitization.

Real-World Examples of Data Validation and Sanitization Failures

SQL Injection Attacks: In 2011, an SQL injection vulnerability in the Sony PlayStation Network led to a massive data breach, exposing personal information of millions of users. This incident highlighted the catastrophic consequences of neglecting proper data validation and sanitization.

XSS Vulnerabilities: In 2017, researchers discovered XSS vulnerabilities in various web applications that allowed attackers to hijack user sessions and steal sensitive information. These vulnerabilities arose from insufficient input sanitization and a lack of encoding special characters.

By understanding and implementing effective validation and sanitization techniques, developers can significantly reduce the risk of data breaches and other security threats. In doing so, they not only enhance the security posture of their applications but also foster user trust and confidence in their services. As we move to the next chapter, we will examine the intricacies of authentication and authorization in web security, further deepening our understanding of secure web application design.

Validating User Input in Go

In this chapter, we will explore the various techniques and tools for validating user input in the Go programming language. We will cover the importance of input validation, common validation techniques, and provide practical examples illustrating how to implement these techniques in Go.

1. The Importance of Input Validation Input validation serves several purposes:
Security: By ensuring that user input conforms to expected formats and ranges, we can protect our

applications from malicious users who may attempt to exploit vulnerabilities (e.g., injection attacks).

Data Integrity: Validating input helps guarantee that the data stored in databases or processed by applications is of high quality and adheres to the expected schema.

User Experience: Providing feedback to users about their input can improve the overall experience. Users are less likely to encounter errors if their inputs are validated in real-time.

2. Common Input Validation Techniques

When validating user input, several common techniques can be utilized:

Type Checking: Ensuring that the data type of the input matches the expected type (e.g., strings, integers, booleans).

Length Checking: Validating that the input falls within a specified length range (e.g., passwords should have a minimum and maximum length).

Format Checking: Using regular expressions or other techniques to ensure the input adheres to a specific format (e.g., email addresses, phone numbers).

Range Checking: Validating that numerical inputs fall within a specific range (e.g., age should be between 0 and 120).

Whitelist and Blacklist Validation: Allowing only specific inputs (whitelisting) or disallowing certain inputs (blacklisting).

3. Built-in and Third-party Libraries for Validation in Go

Go provides several built-in capabilities for input validation, but there are also third-party libraries that can simplify the process. Below are a few notable options:

A. The `net/mail` Package

For validating email addresses, Go offers the `net/mail` package, which provides functionality to parse and validate email formats.

B. Regular Expressions

The `regexp` package can be used for more complex format validations. Regular expressions are powerful tools for parsing and validating string input.

C. Third-party Libraries

There are several popular third-party libraries that simplify input validation:

govalidator: A library that offers functions for string validation and filtering.

validator: A popular library that provides a way to define validation rules using struct tags. ## 4. Practical

Examples
Let's dive into some practical examples that illustrate how to validate user input in Go. ### Example 1: Validating Email Addresses

```go
package main

import (
"fmt" "net/mail"
)

func main() {
email := "user@example.com"

_, err := mail.ParseAddress(email)if err != nil {
fmt.Println("Invalid email address:", err)
} else {
fmt.Println("Valid email address:", email)
}
}
```

In this example, we use the `net/mail` package to validate an email address. If the address is not valid, an error will be returned.

Example 2: Validating User Input with Regular Expressions

```go
package main

import (
```

```go
    "fmt" "regexp"
)

func main() {
    password := "P@ssword123!"

    isValid := validatePassword(password)if isValid {
    fmt.Println("Valid password.")
    } else {
    fmt.Println("Invalid password.")

    }
}

func validatePassword(password string) bool {
    // At least 8 characters, at least one uppercase letter, one
    lowercase letter, one number, and one specialcharacter
    re     :=     regexp.MustCompile(`^(?=.*[a-z])(?=.*[A-
    Z])(?=.*\d)(?=.*[@$!%*?&])[A-Za-z\d@$!%*?&]{8,}$`)
    return re.MatchString(password)
    }
```

This example demonstrates password validation using regular expressions. The regular expression checks for passwords that meet specific criteria, such as length and the inclusion of different character types.

Example 3: Using Struct Tags with the Validator Library We will use the `validator` library to validate struct fields.
First, install the library:

```bash
go get github.com/go-playground/validator/v10
```

Then, implement the validation:

```go
package main

import (
"fmt"
"log"

"github.com/go-playground/validator/v10"
)

type User struct {
Email string `validate:"required,email"`
Username string `validate:"required,min=3,max=30"`
Password                                    string
`validate:"required,min=8,containsany=0123456789"`
}

func main() { user := User{
Email:"user@example.com",Username: "u",
Password: "password",
}

validate := validator.New() err := validate.Struct(user) if
err != nil {
if _, ok := err.(*validator.InvalidValidationError); ok {

log.Println(err)return
```

```
}

for _, err := range err.(validator.ValidationErrors) {
fmt.Printf("Validation    failed    on    field    '%s':    %s\n",
err.StructField(), err.Tag())
}
} else {
fmt.Println("User input is valid.")
}
}
```
```

In this example, we create a `User` struct with validation rules specified using struct tags. The `validator` library checks if the input meets these rules and reports any validation errors.

Validating user input is an essential practice in Go applications, enhancing security, data integrity, and user experience. By utilizing the built-in capabilities of Go alongside powerful third-party libraries, developers can efficiently implement robust validation mechanisms. As you continue to build applications in Go, remember that comprehensive input validation is key to producing reliable and secure software.

## Avoiding Cross-Site Scripting (XSS) Attacks in Go

An XSS attack occurs when an attacker injects malicious scripts into content that is then delivered to users, potentially allowing the attacker to manipulate or steal sensitive information from the user's session, or perform actions on their behalf. Given the growing reliance on web
```

applications built with languages such asGo (Golang), it's essential for developers to understand how to effectively prevent XSS vulnerabilities.

Understanding XSS

Before diving into prevention strategies, it's important to understand how XSS works and its different types:

Stored XSS: The attacker injects a malicious script into a web application, which is then stored (forexample, in a database) and served to users later when they access a particular page.

Reflected XSS: In this scenario, the script is reflected off a web server, typically via a URL queryparameter. If an unsuspecting user clicks on a manipulated link, the malicious script is executed in their browser.

DOM-based XSS: This occurs when the client-side script modifies the DOM environment in a malicious way. The server response does not necessarily contain the malicious code, making it harder todetect.

XSS Prevention Strategies in Go

To effectively guard against XSS attacks in your Go web applications, consider the following strategies: ### 1. Output Encoding
One of the key strategies for preventing XSS is to ensure that all output is properly encoded. This meansconverting characters into a format that will not be interpreted as executable code by the browser.

In Go, you can use the `html` package to help with this:

```go
import (
"html/template"
)

// Example function to safely render user-provided input
func renderTemplate(w http.ResponseWriter, data string) {
tmpl := `
<html>
<body>
<p>User Input: {{.}}</p>
</body>
</html>`

t, err := template.New("webpage").Parse(tmpl)if err != nil {
// handle error
}

if err := t.Execute(w, template.JSEscapeString(data)); err != nil {
// handle error
}
}
```

Using `template.JSEscapeString` helps ensure that any user input is safely rendered without executing any embedded scripts.

126

2. Setting Content Security Policy (CSP)

Content Security Policy (CSP) is a powerful tool to mitigate XSS risks. By specifying which sources of content are trusted, you can restrict executable scripts to only those that you control.

Implementing a CSP in your Go application would typically involve setting HTTP headers:

```go
func setCSPHeader(w http.ResponseWriter) {
w.Header().Set("Content-Security-Policy", "default-src 'self'; script-src 'self'")
}
```

In this example, the CSP directive allows scripts only to be loaded from the same origin (`self`), effectively restricting the execution of any malicious scripts served from external sources.

3. Input Validation

While encoding output is vital, it is equally important to validate input. This includes proper sanitation of any data received from users before it is processed or stored.

Using strict type checks and regular expressions can help ensure the integrity of incoming data:

```go
import (
"regexp"
```

```
)

// Validate simple user input
func isValidInput(input string) bool {
// Simple example: only allow alphanumeric characters
var validInput = regexp.MustCompile(`^[a-zA-Z0-9]+$`)
return validInput.MatchString(input)
}
```

This simple function checks that the input contains only alphanumeric characters, rejecting any potentially harmful attempts to inject scripts.

4. Use Well-maintained Libraries

Utilizing well-maintained and community-approved libraries can significantly reduce the risk of XSS vulnerabilities. The Go community has several libraries that can assist in providing an extra layer of security.

For example, consider using the `gorilla/sessions` package for managing session data as it provides built-in mechanisms to handle data securely.

```go
import (
"github.com/gorilla/sessions"
)

// Create a cookie store for session management
var store = sessions.NewCookieStore([]byte("secret-key"))
```

5. Regular Security Audits

Lastly, incorporating regular security audits into your development process can help you catch potential vulnerabilities early. Tools such as `gosec` or `staticcheck` can analyze your Go code for common securityissues, including XSS vulnerabilities.

```bash
go get -u github.com/securego/gosec/v2/cmd/gosecgosec
./...
```

Running such tools regularly ensures that your application remains pristine and secure from emerging threats.

XSS attacks pose a serious threat to web applications built with Go, but implementing the prevention strategies outlined in this chapter can help developers effectively mitigate these risks. By ensuring properoutput encoding, setting appropriate Content Security Policies, validating input, utilizing well-maintained libraries, and performing regular security audits, you can safeguard your application against XSS vulnerabilities.

Staying informed about the latest security practices and continually refining your approach is necessary in our ever-evolving digital landscape. Prioritizing security during the development process not only protects your application but also fosters user trust and confidence in your product.

Chapter 8: Secure Coding Practices

This chapter delves into the foundational principles and strategies that developers should adopt to build secure applications. By prioritizing security during the coding phase, we can significantly reduce vulnerabilities and protect sensitive data from potential attacks.

8.1 Understanding Security Vulnerabilities

Before diving into secure coding practices, it's vital to understand common security vulnerabilities that can plague software applications. Familiarity with these vulnerabilities enables developers to write code that anticipates and mitigates potential security risks. Some of the most prevalent vulnerabilities include:

Injection flaws: Such as SQL injection, where an attacker can execute arbitrary SQL code through unsanitized inputs.
Cross-Site Scripting (XSS): This occurs when an application allows users to inject malicious scripts into web pages viewed by other users.
Cross-Site Request Forgery (CSRF): A malicious exploit that tricks a user into executing unwanted actions on a web application where they are authenticated.
Insecure Deserialization: This vulnerability arises when untrusted data leading to application logic flaws is deserialized without validation.

Recognizing these vulnerabilities is the first step towards writing secure code.## 8.2 Principles of Secure Coding
Adopting secure coding principles can help developers

create applications that withstand potential attacks. Key principles include:

8.2.1 Least Privilege

Employ the principle of least privilege by ensuring that users and systems have only the minimum permissions necessary to perform their functions. This reduces the attack surface and minimizes the potentialdamage from a compromised account.

8.2.2 Defense in Depth

Utilizing multiple layers of security can help protect applications. If one layer is breached, additional layerscan still provide protection. This includes network security measures, authentication methods, and application security practices.

8.2.3 Input Validation and Output Encoding

Always validate and sanitize user inputs. This practice helps prevent injection attacks and ensures that the application processes only expected and safe data. Additionally, encoding outputs can prevent XSS attacksby ensuring that user-generated content is rendered safely.

8.2.4 Error Handling and Logging

Effective error handling is crucial. Do not expose sensitive information through error messages. Instead, provide user-friendly messages while logging detailed error information for internal review. This protects sensitive data and aids troubleshooting.

8.3 Secure Coding Practices by Language

Different programming languages may have unique considerations when it comes to secure coding. Here, we explore secure coding practices specific to popular languages:

8.3.1 Secure Coding in Java

Use Prepared Statements: To prevent SQL injection, always use parameterized queries or preparedstatements when interacting with databases.
Avoid Default Credentials: Change default usernames and passwords for applications and databasespromptly.

8.3.2 Secure Coding in JavaScript

Sanitize User Input: Libraries like DOMPurify can help sanitize HTML and prevent XSS attacks.
Use Content Security Policy (CSP): Implementing a CSP can prevent the execution of maliciousscripts.

8.3.3 Secure Coding in Python

Utilize Libraries Securely: Use well-maintained libraries and frameworks that have built-in security features (e.g., Django's security middleware).
Validate All Inputs: Use libraries such as WTForms or Django forms to validate and filter inputseffectively.

8.4 Automated Security Tools

Incorporating automated tools into the development process can help identify security issues early on. Examples of tools include:

Static Application Security Testing (SAST): Tools like SonarQube and Checkmarx analyze code at rest for potential security vulnerabilities.
Dynamic Application Security Testing (DAST): These tools, such as OWASP ZAP, evaluate runningapplications for security flaws while they are operational.

8.4.1 Continuous Integration and Testing

Integrating security testing into Continuous Integration/Continuous Deployment (CI/CD) pipelines ensures that security checks are conducted on a regular basis, allowing developers to identify and remedy vulnerabilities quickly.

8.5 Security Awareness and Best Practices

Developers must cultivate a security mindset. Regular training and awareness programs can ensure that theteam stays informed about the latest security trends and practices. Here are some best practices:

Regularly Update Libraries and Frameworks: Keeping libraries updated helps to mitigate knownvulnerabilities.
Adopt Secure Coding Standards: Establishing coding standards that emphasize security can guidedevelopers in their daily work.
Conduct Code Reviews: Implement peer reviews

focusing on security aspects to catch vulnerabilitiesbefore deployment.

Secure coding practices are an integral part of modern software development. By understanding common vulnerabilities, applying fundamental principles of security, leveraging specific coding practices across languages, and utilizing automated tools, developers can significantly enhance the security posture of their applications. As technology continues to evolve, so too must our approaches to coding securely—ensuringthat we are not only building functional applications but also resilient ones that protect user data and maintain trust in our digital ecosystem.

Writing Defensive Code in Go

Defensive programming is a methodology designed to improve the reliability of software by anticipating potential problems and addressing them before they escalate. In this chapter, we will explore the principles of defensive programming in the Go programming language, discussing practical strategies, patterns, and best practices to write code that is not only functional but also resilient.

Understanding Defensive Programming

Defensive programming is based on the idea that developers should safeguard their code from inevitable errors, misuse, and unexpected input. By adopting a defensive approach, developers can reduce the risk of bugs, crashes, and security vulnerabilities. Here are some key principles to keep in mind:

Anticipate Errors: Always consider how users might misuse your code. Be prepared for incorrect inputs, unexpected behaviors, and resource limitations.

Validate Input: Before processing any data, validate it thoroughly. This includes checking for nil pointers, out-of-bounds array accesses, and ensuring that types match expected values.

Use Error Handling: Go emphasizes a robust error-handling mechanism. Never ignore errors; instead, return them to the caller or handle them appropriately within the function.

Encapsulate State: Keep code modular and encapsulate the state wherever possible. This minimizes the risk of unintended side effects from external changes.

Document Assumptions: Clearly document any assumptions your code relies upon. This helps others (and your future self) understand the intent and limitations of the code.

Write Tests: Implement unit tests and integration tests to cover various scenarios, including edge cases.

Strategies for Writing Defensive Go Code ### 1. Input Validation
One of the cornerstones of defensive programming is validating inputs. In Go, this can be accomplished using conditional checks, regular expressions, and the `errors` package.

136

```go
package main

import ( "errors""fmt"
)

// Add function takes two integers and returns their sum
or an error if inputs are invalid. func Add(a, b int) (int,
error) {
if a < 0 || b < 0 {
return 0, errors.New("input values must be non-
negative")
}

return a + b, nil
}

func main() {
result, err := Add(10, -5)if err != nil {
fmt.Println("Error:", err)
} else {
fmt.Println("Result:", result)
}
}
```

2. Robust Error Handling

Go's idiomatic way of handling errors is to return an error
as the last return value. This design encourages developers
to check for errors explicitly at every level of function
calls.

137

```go
func ReadFile(filename string) (string, error) {data, err :=
os.ReadFile(filename)
if err != nil {
return "", fmt.Errorf("failed to read file %s: %w",
filename, err)
}
return string(data), nil
}
```

3. Safe Concurrency

When dealing with concurrency in Go, use channels,
mutexes, and other synchronization primitives from the
`sync` package to manage shared state safely.

```go
type Counter struct {mu    sync.Mutex count int
}

func (c *Counter) Increment() {c.mu.Lock()
defer c.mu.Unlock()c.count++
}

func (c *Counter) Value() int {c.mu.Lock()
defer c.mu.Unlock()return c.count
}
```

4. Graceful Degradation

In some cases, the system may not be able to fulfill a request due to resource limitations or other failures. Implementing graceful degradation ensures that your application still operates under such scenarios, often by providing fallback mechanisms or default values.

```go
func FetchData(url string) ([]byte, error) {response, err :=
http.Get(url)
if err != nil {
// Fallback to a local cache return LoadFromCache(url)
}
defer response.Body.Close()

if response.StatusCode != http.StatusOK {
return nil, fmt.Errorf("failed to fetch data: %s",
response.Status)
}
return io.ReadAll(response.Body)
}
```

5. Testing for Edge Cases

Testing is a critical aspect of defensive programming. Write comprehensive test cases that cover not only the expected inputs but also edge cases. Use table-driven tests to efficiently test multiple scenarios.

```go
func TestAdd(t *testing.T) {tests := []struct {
a, b int result int err error
}{
```

```
{1, 2, 3, nil},
{-1, 1, 0, errors.New("input values must be non-
negative")},
{0, 0, 0, nil},
}

for _, test := range tests {
res, err := Add(test.a, test.b)
if res != test.result || (err != nil && err.Error() !=
test.err.Error()) {
t.Errorf("Add(%d, %d) = %d, %v; want %d, %v", test.a,
test.b, res, err, test.result, test.err)
}
}
}
```

By following the principles and strategies outlined in this chapter—like anticipating errors, validating input, handling errors effectively, ensuring safe concurrency, providing graceful degradation, and thoroughly testing code—you contribute to a codebase that is easier to maintain, debug, and secure. As you write your Go applications, keep these practices in mind to foster an environment of reliability and robustness, benefiting both you and your users.

Avoiding Common Pitfalls in Go Web Applications

This chapter focuses on common pitfalls that developers

might encounter when building web applications with Go, along with strategies to avoid them. Identifying these pitfalls early in the development process can save time, prevent bugs, and lead to more maintainable, efficient applications.

1. Ignoring Error Handling### The Issue
Go is known for its explicit error handling. However, many developers, especially those transitioning from languages with exceptions, underestimate the importance of handling errors correctly. Ignoring errors or handling them ineffectively can lead to unexpected behaviors and security vulnerabilities in web applications.

Solution

Always check for errors and handle them gracefully. This means not just checking for errors returned from functions but also providing meaningful responses to the user and logging errors for further investigation.

```go
result, err := someFunction()if err != nil {
log.Printf("Error occurred: %v", err)
http.Error(w,     "Internal     Server     Error",
http.StatusInternalServerError)return
}
```

2. Poor Concurrency Management### The Issue
Go's concurrency model is one of its strongest features. However, improper use of goroutines and channels can lead to race conditions, deadlocks, or increased memory

usage. This is especially problematic in web applications, where performance directly impacts user experience.

Solution

Utilize the `sync` package to manage shared resources and ensure proper synchronization between goroutines. Consider using context (from the `context` package) to manage cancellation and deadlines in concurrent operations.

```go
var mu sync.Mutex

func safeIncrement() {mu.Lock()
defer mu.Unlock()
// Increment shared counter
}
```

3. Not Following the Idiomatic Go Practices ### The Issue
Go has its idioms and conventions that make the code more readable and maintainable. Developers coming from different programming backgrounds may overlook these idiomatic practices, leading to less effective Go code.

Solution

Familiarize yourself with Go's conventions regarding naming, structuring packages, and writing tests. Use tools like `golint` and `go vet` to ensure your code adheres to idiomatic practices, leading to higher-qualityapplications.

4. Overlooking Security Considerations ### The Issue
Web applications are often targets for various security
vulnerabilities. Go's standard library includes many
utilities for security, but overlooking them or failing to
implement proper security practices can expose
applications to risks such as SQL injection, cross-site
scripting (XSS), and insufficient input validation.

Solution

Sanitize User Input: Always validate and sanitize
input from users. Use libraries such as `html` to escape
potential XSS attacks.

Use Prepared Statements: If you are working with
databases, always use prepared statements to defend
against SQL injection.

Implement Proper Authentication: Use the
`golang.org/x/crypto/bcrypt` library for password
hashing and consider frameworks like `jwt-go` for token-
based authentication.

Keep Dependencies Updated: Regularly update your
dependencies to incorporate the latest securitypatches.

5. Ineffective Logging and Monitoring ### The Issue
Effective logging and monitoring are crucial for
identifying bottlenecks, debugging issues, and keeping
trackof application health. Some developers either log too
much, creating excessive noise, or too little, leading to a

lack of insights.

Solution

Implement structured logging using libraries like `logrus` or `zap`. Log relevant information at appropriate levels (info, warn, error) and avoid logging sensitive user data. Additionally, consider integrating monitoring solutions, such as Prometheus or Grafana, to keep track of application performance and availability.

6. Neglecting Testing and Documentation ### The Issue

Testing helps ensure that your application behaves as expected, while documentation provides guidance for future developers (and yourself). Many developers underestimate the importance of both, leading to technical debt.

Solution

Write Tests: Utilize Go's built-in testing framework to write unit and integration tests. Regularly run your test suite to catch regressions early.

```go
func TestAddition(t *testing.T) {sum := Add(1, 2)
if sum != 3 {
t.Errorf("Expected 3, but got %d", sum)
}
}
```

Document Your Code: Write clear, concise documentation for your code, using Go's doc comments. Organize your project's README file to help others understand its usage and setup.

By being mindful of common pitfalls when building Go web applications, developers can create robust, efficient, and secure applications. Embracing Go's idioms, implementing effective error and concurrency management, ensuring proper security measures, logging, monitoring, testing, and documenting code are vital practices for any mature software engineering process.

Chapter 9: Access Control and Authorization in Web Security

Access control and authorization are critical components of web security that help protect sensitive data and maintain the integrity of web applications. This chapter delves into the principles of access control, the various models and methods employed, and best practices to implement these mechanisms effectively.

Understanding Access Control

Access control refers to the process of determining who can access specific resources in a computing environment. It governs the permissions and privileges of users and ensures that sensitive information is only available to those with the appropriate authorization. Essentially, access control acts as a barrier that guards against unauthorized access and data breaches.

Types of Access Control

Discretionary Access Control (DAC): In DAC systems, the resource owner defines who has access to their resources. This model is flexible, allowing users to share their resources with others but can be prone to security risks due to its reliance on user discretion.

Mandatory Access Control (MAC): In MAC, access rights are assigned based on regulations determined by a central authority. Users cannot alter permissions. This model provides a higher level of security, making it ideal for government and military applications where data sensitivity is critical.

Role-Based Access Control (RBAC): RBAC assigns access permissions based on user roles within an organization. Each role has specific permissions, and users inherit access rights based on the role they are assigned, simplifying the management of permissions in large environments.

Attribute-Based Access Control (ABAC): ABAC allows access decisions based on attributes of the user, resource, and environment conditions. This model offers more granularity and flexibility, enabling organizations to define complex access rules.

The Authorization Process

Authorization is the process that follows authentication, where a user's identity is validated and confirmed. After authentication, the system checks the user's permissions to determine what resources they can access and what actions they can perform. The authorization process typically involves the following steps:

User Authentication: Validate the identity of the user using methods such as passwords, biometrics, tokens, or multi-factor authentication (MFA).

Role Assignment: Assign the authenticated user to a specific role or roles in the system, based on their job function or responsibilities.

147

Policy Enforcement: Utilize access control policies to determine the authorized actions for each user role. The system checks these policies every time an access attempt is made.

Access Decision: The culmination of the above steps leads to an access decision, allowing or denying access based on the defined policies and user permissions.

Implementing Access Control

When implementing access control in web applications, several best practices should be followed: ### 1. Principle of Least Privilege
Users should be granted only the access necessary to perform their jobs. This minimizes the potential damage in case of a compromised account and reduces the attack surface.

2. Regular Audits and Reviews

Conduct regular audits of user roles and permissions to ensure that they align with current responsibilities. This helps identify and revoke any unnecessary access.

3. Use of Strong Authentication Methods

To enhance security, employ strong authentication mechanisms, such as MFA, which requires multiple forms of verification before granting access.

4. Logging and Monitoring

Maintain comprehensive logs of user activities and access attempts. Implement monitoring to detect unusual access patterns that might indicate a security breach.

5. Session Management

Implement effective session management practices, such as session timeouts and secure session tokens, to prevent unauthorized access during user inactivity.

Challenges in Access Control

While access control is essential for web security, it comes with challenges:

Complexity: Organizations may operate in dynamic environments with changing roles and responsibilities, making it difficult to manage access control effectively.

User Behavior: Users may inadvertently share credentials or forget to log out, creating vulnerabilities in access control systems.

Integration: Integrating access control mechanisms with existing systems and applications can be challenging, particularly in legacy environments.

Understanding different access control models, implementing best practices, and addressing inherent challenges can significantly enhance the security posture of web applications. As cyber threats continue to evolve, the importance of robust access control mechanisms cannot be overstated, making it a crucial area of focus for security professionals and organizations alike.

Role-Based Access Control (RBAC) Implementation in Go

One of the most widely adopted methods for controlling access to resources is Role-Based Access Control(RBAC). In this chapter, we'll explore the fundamentals of RBAC and how to implement it in Go, a statically typed, compiled programming language known for its simplicity and efficiency.

What is Role-Based Access Control (RBAC)?

Role-Based Access Control (RBAC) is a method for restricting system access to authorized users based on their assigned roles. A role is defined as a collection of permissions that dictate what resources a user can access and what actions can be performed. By grouping users into roles, RBAC simplifies management and enhances security.

Key Concepts

User: An individual who interacts with the system.
Role: A defined set of permissions associated with a user's job functions.
Permission: The ability to perform a specific action on a resource, such as read, write, or delete.
Resource: An entity within the system, such as a file, directory, or API endpoint.## Benefits of Implementing

RBAC

Simplified Administration: By managing access rights through roles rather than individual user permissions, organizations can streamline user administration processes.

Increased Security: RBAC ensures that users can only access information relevant to their job functions, reducing the risk of unauthorized access.

Auditing and Compliance: With clearly defined roles and permissions, organizations can better track user activities and maintain compliance with regulations.

Design Considerations for RBAC

When implementing RBAC, specific design considerations should be taken into account:

Role Hierarchy: Establishing a hierarchy of roles can simplify management. A senior role may inherit permissions from junior roles.

Dynamic Role Assignment: Providing mechanisms for dynamic role assignment based on user attributes or contextual data can enhance flexibility.

Granular Permissions: Ensuring that permissions are not too broad increases security by maintaining least privilege access.

Implementing RBAC in Go

In this section, we will guide you through the implementation of a simple RBAC system in Go. We will create a basic application that defines users, roles, and permissions with the ability to check access.

Step 1: Define Structures

First, we need to define the basic structures for our users, roles, and permissions.

```go
package main

import "fmt"

// Permission represents the various actions that can be
performed on resources.type Permission string

const (
ReadPermission Permission = "read" WritePermission
Permission = "write" DeletePermission Permission =
"delete"
)

// Role represents a user's role which contains multiple
permissions.type Role struct {
Name string Permissions []Permission
}

// User is an entity carrying information about the user
and their roles.type User struct {
Username stringRoles      []Role
}
```

Step 2: Role and Permission Management

Next, we will create a function to check if a user has a specific permission based on their roles.

```go
// HasPermission checks whether the user has a specific
permission. func (u User) HasPermission(permission
Permission) bool {
for _, role := range u.Roles {
for _, perm := range role.Permissions { if perm ==
permission {
return true
}
}
}
return false
}
```

Step 3: Sample Data

Let's create some sample roles and users.

```go
func main() {
// Define roles adminRole := Role{
Name:"Admin",
Permissions:              []Permission{ReadPermission,
WritePermission, DeletePermission},
}

userRole := Role{ Name:   "User",
Permissions: []Permission{ReadPermission},
}
```

153

```go
// Define usersalice := User{
Username: "Alice",
Roles: []Role{adminRole},
}

bob := User{ Username: "Bob",
Roles: []Role{userRole},
}

// Check permissions checkPermissions(alice)
checkPermissions(bob)
}

// Function to check user permissions func
checkPermissions(user User) {
fmt.Printf("Permissions for %s:\n", user.Username)
permissions := []Permission{ReadPermission,
WritePermission, DeletePermission}for _, perm := range
permissions {
if user.HasPermission(perm) { fmt.Printf("- %s:
Allowed\n", perm)
} else {
fmt.Printf("- %s: Denied\n", perm)
}
}
}
```
```

### Step 4: Testing Access

Now, let's compile and run our Go program. You should
see console output illustrating which permissions each
```

user has:

```
Permissions for Alice:
read: Allowed
write: Allowed
delete: Allowed Permissions for Bob:
read: Allowed
write: Denied
delete: Denied
```

In this chapter, we've introduced the concept of Role-Based Access Control (RBAC) and demonstrated a straightforward implementation in Go. The core elements of user, role, and permission structures provide a robust foundation for managing access across applications. As systems grow in complexity, RBAC can
effectively support security needs while ensuring operational efficiency.

Advanced Authorization Techniques

Websites and web applications are frequent targets for a variety of security threats, and authorization plays a crucial role in safeguarding sensitive data and ensuring that users have appropriate access levels. This chapter delves into advanced authorization techniques for web security, specifically utilizing the Go programming language. By the end of this chapter, you will have a comprehensive understanding of how to implement effective and flexible authorization mechanisms in your web applications.

8.1 Understanding Authorization

Before diving into advanced techniques, it's essential to clarify what authorization is. Authorization is the process that determines whether a user has the right to access certain resources or perform specific actions. While authentication verifies the identity of a user (e.g., logging in with a username and password), authorization is responsible for managing user permissions.

8.1.1 Role-Based Access Control (RBAC)

RBAC is one of the most common models used for managing user permissions. In this model, users are assigned to roles, and each role has a set of permissions to access various system components. For example, in an e-commerce application, you might have three roles: Administrator, Customer, and Guest. Each role has different permissions, allowing for a clear hierarchy of access control.

8.1.2 Attribute-Based Access Control (ABAC)

ABAC extends the concept of RBAC by allowing permissions based on user attributes, resource attributes, and contextual information (like time of access). This approach is more flexible than RBAC as it enables dynamic decision-making based on various factors. For instance, you could allow access to sensitive data based on user location, device type, or security clearance level.

8.2 Implementing RBAC in Go

Now, let's implement a simple RBAC system using Go. We will create a web server that manages user roles and their permissions.

8.2.1 Setting Up the Go Environment

First, ensure that you have Go installed on your machine. You can create a new directory for our project and initialize a Go module.

```bash
mkdir go-rbac-examplecd go-rbac-example
go mod init go-rbac-example
```

8.2.2 Defining Roles and Permissions

Create a structure to define roles and permissions in our application.

```go
package main

import "fmt" type Role string
const (
Admin Role = "admin" User Role = "user" Guest Role = "guest"
)
type Permission stringconst (
Read Permission = "read" Write Permission = "write"
Delete Permission = "delete"
```

157

```go
)

type RolePermission struct {Role Role
Permissions []Permission
}

var rolePermissions = []RolePermission{
{Admin, []Permission{Read, Write, Delete}},
{User, []Permission{Read, Write}},
{Guest, []Permission{Read}},
}
```

8.2.3 Authorization Logic

Now we'll create a function to check user permissions based on roles.

```go
func hasPermission(role Role, permission Permission)
bool {for _, rp := range rolePermissions {
if rp.Role == role {
for _, p := range rp.Permissions {if p == permission {
return true
}
}
}
}
return false
}

func main() { userRole := User
if hasPermission(userRole, Write) { fmt.Println("User has
```

158

```go
write permission.")
} else {
fmt.Println("User does not have write permission.")

}
}
```
```

### 8.2.4 Running the Server

You can create a simple web server to demonstrate role-based access control.

```go
package main

import ( "fmt" "net/http"
)

func restrictedHandler(w http.ResponseWriter, r
*http.Request) {
role := r.Header.Get("Role") // Assume the role is passed
in HTTP headers

if !hasPermission(Role(role), Read) {
http.Error(w, "Forbidden", http.StatusForbidden)return
}

fmt.Fprintln(w, "Welcome to the restricted area!")
}

func main() {
http.HandleFunc("/restricted",        restrictedHandler)
```
```

```go
    http.ListenAndServe(":8080", nil)
}
```

8.3 Attribute-Based Access Control (ABAC) in Go

Next, we will explore how to implement ABAC. The
flexibility of ABAC allows policies to be clearer and more
context-sensitive, but implementing it requires a more
sophisticated approach.

8.3.1 Policy Definitions

ABAC can be applied through policy definitions that
evaluate user and resource attributes. Let's define a simple
structure for our policies.

```go
type Policy struct { UserAttributes map[string]string
ResourceAttributes map[string]stringAction Permission
Allowed bool
}

var policies = []Policy{
{
UserAttributes: map[string]string{"role": "admin"},

ResourceAttributes: map[string]string{"resourceType":
"sensitive"},Action: Write,
Allowed: true,
},
{
UserAttributes:    map[string]string{"role":    "user"},
```
160

```go
ResourceAttributes:   map[string]string{"resourceType":
"sensitive"},Action: Write,
Allowed: false,
},
}
```

8.3.2 Policy Evaluation Function

Next, we implement a function to evaluate a policy based
on user and resource attributes.

```go
func  evaluatePolicy(userAttributes  map[string]string,
resourceAttributes map[string]string, action Permission)
bool {
for _, policy := range policies {
if        policy.Action        ==        action        &&
compareAttributes(userAttributes, policy.UserAttributes)
&&              compareAttributes(resourceAttributes,
policy.ResourceAttributes) {
return policy.Allowed
}
}
return false
}

func       compareAttributes(userAttrs,       policyAttrs
map[string]string) bool {for k, v := range policyAttrs {
if userAttrs[k] != v {return false
}
}
return true
```

161

```
}
```

8.3.3 Implementing ABAC in a Web Server

Finally, let's connect our ABAC implementation with a simple web server.

```go
func abacHandler(w http.ResponseWriter, r *http.Request) { userAttributes := map[string]string{"role": r.Header.Get("Role")}
resourceAttributes := map[string]string{"resourceType": "sensitive"}action := Write

if !evaluatePolicy(userAttributes, resourceAttributes, action) {http.Error(w, "Forbidden", http.StatusForbidden)
return
}

fmt.Fprintln(w, "User is allowed to perform the action.")
}

func main() {
http.HandleFunc("/abac", abacHandler)
http.ListenAndServe(":8080", nil)
}
```

As threats evolve and user needs change, continue to explore and implement advanced security measures and best practices, keeping your systems safe and secure in an ever-changing digital landscape. The speed and efficiency of the Go programming language make it an excellent choice for these implementations. Always be prepared to review and refine authorization strategies to keep pace with new security challenges.

Chapter 10: Securing Third-Party Integrations

From payment gateways and content delivery networks (CDNs) to analytics tools and social media logins, these integrations undoubtedly add powerful capabilities to web applications. However, they also introduce significant security vulnerabilities that can jeopardize the integrity of systems and the privacy of users. This chapter explores the critical aspects of securing third-party integrations in web security, outlining best practices, common threats, and effective strategies for mitigating risks.

Understanding Third-Party Integrations

Third-party integrations refer to the use of external systems or services that interact with a primary application or platform. These could involve APIs, SDKs (Software Development Kits), plugins, or libraries that allow applications to communicate with external services. While these integrations can provide valuable features— such as real-time data sharing, user authentication, and enhanced functionality—they also entail inherent risks due to the lack of direct control over the third-party software and the data transmitted between systems.

Common Threats and Vulnerabilities ### 1. **Data Exposure**
When integrating third-party services, sensitive data may be transmitted over the network. If not properly secured, this data can be intercepted by malicious actors. Additionally, vulnerabilities in the third-party service's

API can lead to unauthorized access and data breaches.

2. **Dependency Risks**

Applications relying on third-party services may become vulnerable if those services are compromised. For example, if a popular authentication service suffers a security breach, all applications that utilize that service may be at risk, even if they have robust security measures in place.

3. **Supply Chain Attacks**

Cybercriminals may target third-party libraries or services to inject malicious code that could compromise connected applications. This type of attack exploits the trust relationship between the main application and the third-party service.

4. **Insufficient Security Measures**

Many developers assume that third-party services automatically implement strong security practices. However, this is not always the case. If the third-party service lacks necessary protections such as encryption, secure storage, and proper access controls, the integrating application can inherit these vulnerabilities.

Best Practices for Securing Third-Party Integrations
1. **Conduct Risk Assessments**
Before integrating with any third-party service, conduct a comprehensive risk assessment to evaluate the potential security implications. Understand the data being

exchanged, the potential vulnerabilities, and the implications of a breach.

2. **Use Secure Connections**

Always utilize HTTPS (Hypertext Transfer Protocol Secure) to encrypt data in transit between your application and third-party services. This prevents data interception through man-in-the-middle attacks and ensures that user data remains confidential.

3. **Implement Authentication and Authorization**

When integrating third-party services, implement robust authentication and authorization processes. Use OAuth or similar protocols to ensure that only authorized users and applications can access sensitive data and functionality.

4. **Regularly Review Third-Party Services**

Perform regular audits of third-party services and keep track of any reported vulnerabilities or breaches. If a service has a history of security issues or does not meet industry standards, consider alternatives or reducing integration dependencies.

5. **Limit Data Scope**

Only share necessary data with third-party services, adhering to the principle of least privilege. This minimizes potential exposure in the event of a breach. For instance, if a service only needs a user's email address, avoid sharing more sensitive details such as their full name or address.

6. **Monitor and Log Activities**

Implement robust logging and monitoring for third-party interactions. This allows for the detection of unusual behavior that may indicate compromise, data leaks, or unauthorized access attempts. Use centralized logging solutions to aggregate and analyze logs from various integrations.

7. **Maintain Version Control**

Regularly update any third-party libraries, SDKs, and APIs to ensure you're using the latest secure versions. Outdated software can contain known vulnerabilities that are easily exploited. Implement dependency management tools to automate version updates.

8. **Establish an Incident Response Plan**

Have a well-defined incident response plan in place to address potential security breaches related to third-party integrations. This plan should include steps for containment, investigation, communication, and remediation.

Case Studies

Case Study 1: The Payment Gateway Breach

In 2019, a major e-commerce platform suffered a data breach when a widely used payment gateway was compromised. The attackers exploited vulnerabilities in the gateway's API to siphon off credit card information from customers. The e-commerce platform had relied heavily on the payment service without conducting adequate due diligence, primarily trusting that the service maintained high security standards. The aftermath involved significant financial loss, reputational damage, and regulatory scrutiny.

Case Study 2: Insufficient Data Sharing

A healthcare application integrated with a third-party analytics service to enhance user engagement. However, the analytics service inadvertently exposed sensitive user health records due to misconfigured access controls. The breach raised serious privacy concerns and led to regulatory penalties. The healthcare provider learned the hard way the importance of limiting shared data scope and conducting thorough security reviews of integrations.

By recognizing potential threats and implementing effective strategies, organizations can significantly mitigate risks associated with third-party services. Remember that security is a shared responsibility; while integrating with external services brings many benefits, it is crucial to ensure that these services are secure and that their integration does not compromise the integrity of your application or the safety of user data. Effective security measures, continuous monitoring, and adherence to best practices are essential in today's increasingly interconnected web environment.

Safely Integrating External Libraries and APIs

While Go (or Golang) provides a robust environment for building applications, integrating external libraries and APIs safely requires careful consideration. In this chapter, we will explore how to effectively and safely integrate third-party libraries and APIs in your Go applications while addressing potential risks such as security vulnerabilities, compatibility issues, and maintainability challenges.

Understanding External Libraries and APIs ### What are External Libraries?
External libraries are packages that contain reusable code written by other developers, which can be imported into your Go project. Libraries can range from simple utility packages to complex frameworks that provide extensive functionality. They are typically shared through repositories like GitHub or Go's own package management system, `go get`.

What are APIs?

APIs (Application Programming Interfaces) provide a set of rules and protocols for building and interacting with software applications. External APIs allow your applications to communicate with other services over the internet, retrieving or sending data without needing to know the implementation details. APIs can expose functionality such as payment processing, user authentication, data storage, or even machine learning capabilities.

The Risks of Integrating External Libraries and APIs

While integrating external libraries and APIs can enhance functionality, it also introduces risks:

Security Vulnerabilities: Third-party libraries can harbor security flaws that expose your application to potential attacks. If an external library is compromised, your application may also be at risk.

Dependency Management: Managing versions and dependencies across multiple libraries can become tedious, potentially leading to conflicts or breaking changes.

Performance Issues: Some libraries may not be optimized for your specific use case, leading to unnecessary overhead or degraded application performance.

Lack of Documentation: The absence of clear and up-to-date documentation can lead to misunderstandings in how to properly utilize a library or API, resulting in bugs or inefficiencies.

Abandonment: A library that is no longer actively maintained can become a liability, as updates for bug fixes or new features may not be forthcoming.

Best Practices for Safely Integrating External Libraries
1. Evaluate Libraries
Before incorporating any library, conduct a thorough evaluation:

Popularity and Community Support: Check how widely used the library is. Popular libraries usually have better community support, which translates to a higher likelihood of bug fixes and feature updates.
Audit the Code: If possible, review the source code of the library for any potential vulnerabilities.

Open-source libraries allow you to do this easily.
Check the License: Ensure the library's license aligns with your project's requirements, especially in commercial applications.

2. Version Control

Use Go modules for version control of libraries:

Semantic Versioning: Be aware of how versions are controlled. Prefer libraries that follow semantic versioning (semver), as it gives you some assurance about the maturity and stability of the library.
Update Regularly: Keep your dependencies updated to benefit from bug fixes and security patches. Use tools like Go's built-in dependency management commands (e.g., `go get -u`) to streamline this process.

3. Isolate Dependencies

Use Dependency Injection: Utilize design patterns that allow you to inject dependencies instead of hardcoding them. This promotes testability and ease of swapping libraries.
Docker Containerization: In environments where

dependency isolation is critical, consider using Docker containers to encapsulate your application and its dependencies.

4. Implement Robust Error Handling

Graceful Degradation: Instead of allowing your application to fail when an external API call does not respond or a library throws an error, implement error handling that allows your application to continue functioning, perhaps by providing fallback content or functionality.
Logging: Make sure to log errors from external library calls. This practice not only aids in troubleshooting but also helps identify problematic integrations.

Best Practices for Safely Integrating External APIs ### 1. API Keys and Secrets Management
Secure Storage: Store API keys and other sensitive information securely using environment variables or secret management tools instead of hardcoding them into your application.
Least Privilege Principle: Only use the minimum required permissions needed for your API access. ### 2. Rate Limiting and Throttling
Understand the limits imposed by external APIs and design your application to handle rate limits. This can help avoid unexpected service disruptions due to exceeding allowed requests.

3. Use API Client Libraries

If available, leverage API client libraries created for the

language you are using. These libraries often handle various complexities like authentication, error handling, and request structuring for you.

4. Monitor and Test

Monitoring: Implement monitoring for API usage and performance. Being able to visualize API performance over time is essential in identifying potential issues.
Testing: Use mock servers or stubs while testing your application to simulate API responses, ensuring that your code behaves as expected without hitting live endpoints during the testing phase.

Managing Dependency Vulnerabilities

Dependency vulnerabilities pose significant risks, potentially opening doors for exploitation. This chapter delves into the landscape of dependency vulnerabilities in Go, exploring best practices for vulnerability management, tools for detection, and strategies for remediating risks.

Understanding Dependency Vulnerabilities ### What are Dependency Vulnerabilities?
Dependency vulnerabilities occur when an external library or package contains flaws, security loopholes, or outdated components that can be exploited by malicious actors. These vulnerabilities can range from minor bugs to critical security issues that could compromise the entire application. Given that modern applications often consist

of innumerable dependencies, it becomes paramount to understand and manage these vulnerabilities effectively.

Common Causes of Vulnerabilities

Outdated Dependencies: Libraries evolve over time, and older versions often contain unpatched security vulnerabilities.
Transitive Dependencies: A package might rely on other packages which may themselves have vulnerabilities. These are often overlooked and can lead to cascading security risks.
Incomplete Security Audits: Not all libraries undergo rigorous security assessments, leaving potential flaws unnoticed.

Tools for Managing Dependencies

Go offers a robust ecosystem of tools that assist developers in managing their dependencies effectively. Below are some of the essential tools for vulnerability management:

1. Go Modules

Go modules, introduced in Go 1.11, simplify dependency management and help ensure that your application relies on the intended versions of packages. By using `go.mod` and `go.sum` files, developers can specify exact versions of dependencies and their checksums, providing an additional layer of verification.

2. `go get` and Versioning

Using the `go get` command not only enables developers to fetch dependencies but also allows them to update them securely. It is advised to regularly run `go get -u` to fetch the latest minor and patch releases of dependencies, which may include security updates.

3. Vulnerability Scanning Tools

Several tools can automatically scan your dependencies for known vulnerabilities:

Snyk: A developer-first security platform that integrates with Go projects to identify vulnerabilities across the dependency tree.
Dependabot: A GitHub feature that automatically suggests updates to dependencies in your project, highlighting known security vulnerabilities.
Goscan: A Go-specific vulnerability scanning tool that checks for known vulnerabilities in Go libraries.

4. Static Analysis Tools

Tools like `golint`, `staticcheck`, and `gosec` help in identifying potential vulnerabilities in the codebase, enabling developers to catch issues before they result in security breaches.

Best Practices for Managing Vulnerabilities ### 1. Regular Dependency Audits
Conduct regular audits of dependencies to identify outdated or vulnerable components. Engage in proactive monitoring to catch vulnerabilities early. Consider setting

up automated scripts to run vulnerability scans on a scheduled basis.

2. Update Policies

Establish clear policies for updating dependencies. Consider using tools like Dependabot or Renovate for automated pull requests that prompt you to update vulnerable packages. Create a process for regularly reviewing and testing updates, especially for major version changes that could introduce breaking changes.

3. Utilize an Approval Workflow

For critical applications, especially in production environments, implement an approval workflow for dependency updates. Ensure that any third-party code introduced to your repository undergoes a securityreview.

4. Adopt a Defense-in-Depth Strategy

Implement security layers, such as network security measures, access controls, and input validation, toprovide multiple barriers against potential exploitation.

5. Stay Informed

Stay informed about vulnerabilities by subscribing to security mailing lists, joining developer communities, or following dedicated security research groups. Awareness is key to managing risks and ensuring timely updates to addresses vulnerabilities.

Remediation Strategies

When a vulnerability is identified, immediate action is crucial. Below are some recommended strategies for remediation:

1. Evaluate and Prioritize

Assess the severity of the identified vulnerability. Critical vulnerabilities that can lead to remote code execution should be prioritized over lower-severity issues. Use CVSS (Common Vulnerability Scoring System) scores to help prioritize remediation efforts.

2. Upgrade or Patch

The first step in remediation often involves upgrading the vulnerable package. Refer to the package's documentation for recommended fixes or patches. If an immediate upgrade isn't possible, evaluate if the vulnerable component can be replaced with an alternative.

3. Code Review and Testing

After remediation, conduct thorough code reviews and testing to ensure that the fix works as intended and does not introduce new issues. Automated tests, especially unit tests, can be beneficial in this phase.

4. Document Vulnerability Management

Maintain records of identified vulnerabilities, resolutions, and the decision-making process behind fixes.

Documentation aids in understanding historical decisions and can improve the vulnerability management process over time.

Managing dependency vulnerabilities in Go is an ongoing process that demands attention, diligence, and an understanding of best practices. With the right tools and strategies in place, developers can mitigate risks associated with external dependencies, ensuring that their applications remain secure and resilient against potential threats. By fostering a culture of security awareness and proactive vulnerability management, Go developers can protect their applications and deliver high-quality software with confidence.

Chapter 11: Building Resilient Web Applications

A resilient web application is one that can withstand adverse conditions, such as high traffic loads, unexpected failures, and cyber threats, while still delivering a seamless user experience. This chapter explores the principles, strategies, and best practices for building resilient web applications, ensuring they remain robust and reliable in the face of challenges.

1. Understanding Resilience in Web Applications

Resilience describes an application's ability to recover from failures and adapt to changes while maintaining essential functionalities. In the context of web applications, this means providing a consistent user experience, even during outages, high load periods, or security incidents. To build resilience, developers must focus on several key areas:

Fault Tolerance: The application should continue to operate, or at least degrade gracefully, in the event of component failures.
Scalability: Being able to manage increased load without service degradation, whether that's through horizontal scaling (adding more instances) or vertical scaling (enhancing existing resources).
Security: Protecting against attacks and breaches that might compromise the integrity or availability of the application.
Recoverability: Implementing measures that allow for

quick recovery from failures, including automated backups and easy rollbacks.

2. Designing for Fault Tolerance ### 2.1 Redundancy
One of the foundational aspects of building resilient systems is redundancy. This can be implemented at various levels:

Server Redundancy: Deploy applications across multiple servers or containers that can take over in case one fails.
Data Redundancy: Use replicated databases across different geographical locations or cloud regions to protect against data loss.

2.2 Circuit Breaker Pattern

The circuit breaker pattern is an architectural pattern that helps improve the stability of a system by preventing calls to a service that has a high likelihood of failure. If repeated failures occur after a threshold is reached, the circuit breaker will open, temporarily blocking requests to that service. This mechanism allows the system to fail fast and recover more quickly without overwhelming the compromised service.

2.3 Health Checks and Monitoring

Incorporate health checks and monitoring systems to detect failures proactively. This involves setting up automated tools that can track the application's performance and identify anomalies in real time. Alerting mechanisms can notify developers or operations teams when issues arise, allowing for quick interventions before they escalate.

3. Ensuring Scalability ### 3.1 Load Balancing

Load balancing distributes incoming traffic across multiple servers or instances, ensuring no single instance bears too much load. This strategy not only enhances performance but also improves fault tolerance, as it allows traffic to be rerouted if one server fails.

3.2 Statelessness

Design your web applications to be stateless—where the server does not store user session information. By relying on external services (like databases or distributed caches) to maintain state, applications can easily scale horizontally as more instances can be added without concerns about session affinity.

3.3 Caching Strategies

Use caching mechanisms to store frequently accessed data or resources. This can drastically reduce the load on the database and improve the application's response time. Implement caching at various levels, such as client-side, server-side, and CDN (Content Delivery Network).

4. Enhancing Security

4.1 Secure Coding Practices

Start with secure coding practices that protect against

common vulnerabilities, such as SQL injection, cross-site scripting (XSS), and buffer overflow attacks. Use security libraries and frameworks that provide built-inprotections against many common threats.

4.2 Regular Security Audits

Conduct regular security reviews and penetration testing to identify and rectify vulnerabilities within your application. This proactive approach helps in grounding the application in security best practices and compliance with regulations.

4.3 Incident Response Plan

Even with robust security measures in place, breaches can occur. Establish an incident response plan that outlines procedures for detection, response, and recovery following a security incident. This includes communication plans, identification of roles, and escalation processes.

5. Implementing Recovery Measures ### 5.1 Automated Backups
Implement automated backup solutions that regularly back up data and application states. Ensure that these backups are stored in different locations and can be restored quickly in case of data loss events.

5.2 Disaster Recovery Planning

A comprehensive disaster recovery plan is essential for business continuity. This plan should outline how to quickly restore services in the event of catastrophic failures, including data recovery, server infrastructure provisioning, and application re-deployment strategies.

5.3 Progressive Deployment

Utilize progressive deployment strategies, such as blue-green deployments or canary releases, to minimize risks associated with new releases. This allows you to test new features with a subset of users and roll back quickly if issues arise.

By adopting a proactive mindset and leveraging modern technologies, you can create web applications that not only meet user expectations but also thrive in the face of adversity. As user demands and threats continue to evolve, resilience will remain a critical pillar in the ongoing development of robust web applications.

Error Handling and Logging Best Practices

The way developers handle errors significantly influences the user experience, system stability, and maintainability of applications. In this chapter, we will explore best practices for error handling and logging, ensuring robust, maintainable, and user-friendly software.

1. Understand Different Types of Errors

Errors can be categorized into several types, and recognizing these can guide developers in implementing effective error handling:

a. Syntax Errors
These are mistakes in the code syntax that prevent the program from compiling. Syntax errors are usually caught during the compilation or interpretation of the code and are often straightforward to fix.

b. Runtime Errors
Unlike syntax errors, runtime errors occur during program execution. These could be due to null references, out-of-bounds access, or issues like division by zero. Developing a strategy for managing runtime errors is crucial for maintaining application stability.

c. Logical Errors
Logical errors are subtler, as the program compiles and runs without issue, but produces incorrect results. These require a different strategy focused on thorough testing and validation of the program's logic.

d. External Errors
These occur due to factors outside the application, such as file not found errors, network timeouts, or database connection issues. Effective error handling must consider external dependencies to gracefully manage failures.

2. Implementing Effective Error Handling

a. Use Try-Catch Blocks Wisely
One of the most common structures for error handling is the try-catch block. However, its misuse can lead to poor code and obscure bugs. Use try-catch sparingly for areas of code where you anticipate potential errors, and avoid using it to control the flow of logic.

b. Specific Error Handling

Catch specific exceptions and handle them accordingly. This provides clearer error messages and allows for tailored responses based on the type of error. Avoid catching general exceptions unless you are sure about the context and can handle them appropriately.

c. Avoid Silent Failures
When an error occurs, it is crucial not to ignore it. Instead, ensure that your application can log the error, notify users when appropriate, and allow for recovery or remediation.

d. Graceful Degradation
In cases of failure, aim for graceful degradation, where the application continues operating in a limited capacity rather than crashing outright. Provide users with meaningful feedback or alternative actions.

3. Logging Best Practices

Logging is integral to error handling, providing valuable data for diagnosing and fixing issues. Here are some best practices for effective logging:

a. Use a Logging Framework
Take advantage of logging libraries or frameworks that can help structure and manage log outputs. Popular choices include Log4j for Java, NLog for .NET, and Winston for Node.js. They often provide features such as varying log levels, output formatting, and integration with external systems.

b. Log Levels
Implement various logging levels—such as DEBUG, INFO,

WARN, ERROR, and FATAL—to categorize log entries. This allows developers to filter logs based on severity and focus on critical issues, especially during troubleshooting.

c. Include Contextual Information
When logging errors, include contextual information such as method names, parameters, user IDs, andtimestamps. This data enhances the ability to trace the root cause of an issue and understand the circumstances that led to it.

d. Avoid Logging Sensitive Information
Be cautious not to log sensitive data, such as passwords, personal identification numbers, or credit card information. This is not only a security risk but can also violate privacy regulations.

e. Monitor and Analyze Logs
Implement a system to monitor logs continually. Automated analysis tools can help detect patterns or frequent errors and can alert developers to potential issues before they escalate.

4. Testing and Validation

Testing plays a pivotal role in error handling and logging strategies. Several methods can assure the reliability of your error handling:

a. Unit Tests
Thoroughly test error handling paths with unit tests. Simulate different error scenarios and assert that the application behaves as expected.

b. Integration Tests
Following unit tests, perform integration tests to ensure that the interaction between different components of your system handles errors smoothly.

c. User Acceptance Testing (UAT)
Gather feedback from end-users to further refine error handling. Users are the best source for identifying areas of confusion or frustration during error occurrences.

5. Documentation and Communication
Effective error handling and logging should also involve clear documentation: ### a. Document Error Codes and Messages
Maintain an organized manual of error codes and corresponding messages, providing clarity for both developers and end-users. This helps in understanding the errors that might occur and how to respond.

b. Communication Channels
Set up communication channels, such as issue tracking systems or slack channels for reporting and discussing errors among development teams. This ensures collective knowledge and quicker resolutions.

Error handling and logging are fundamental components of software development that should be approached with care and diligence. By understanding the types of errors, implementing effective error-handling strategies, utilizing best practices for logging, testing, and maintaining clear documentation, developers can create resilient software that not only recovers from errors gracefully but also provides valuable insights for future development.

Graceful Degradation and Recovery Strategies

This chapter explores the concepts of graceful degradation and recovery strategies in system design, focusing on how systems can maintain functionality under stress or partial failures and how they can recover from such incidents.

Understanding Graceful Degradation

Graceful degradation refers to a system's ability to continue functioning, albeit at a reduced level, when parts of the system fail or when it faces certain limitations. This concept ensures that users can still access core functionalities without experiencing complete service failure.

Key Principles of Graceful Degradation

Modularity: Systems should be designed in a modular fashion, allowing individual components to be isolated. If one module fails, others can compensate without affecting overall system performance.

Prioritization of Features: Not all features are created equal. In the event of a failure, prioritizing critical functionalities ensures that the system continues to serve essential user needs.

Fallback Mechanisms: Systems should include alternative processes to take over when primary functions fail. For instance, a web application might offer a simple HTML version if the rich interactive interface becomes unavailable.

User Feedback: Communicating with users during a degradation event is crucial. Systems should provide clear feedback about what functionalities are unavailable and any changes in the user experience.

Examples of Graceful Degradation

In the world of technology, countless examples of graceful degradation can be observed. Streaming services, for instance, often lower video quality and provide lower bandwidth options during network congestion. E-commerce platforms may disable certain high-demand features during peak traffic but still allow customers to browse products and make purchases.

Building Recovery Strategies

When systems encounter failures, recovery strategies are essential for restoring normal functionality. Recovery strategies fall into two main categories: proactive and reactive approaches.

Proactive Recovery Strategies

Redundancy: By having backup systems in place, organizations can continue operations seamlessly. For example, data center infrastructures often include redundant power supplies and network connections.

Regular Maintenance and Testing: Scheduling routine maintenance checks and conducting stress tests help identify vulnerabilities before they lead to failures.

Load Balancing: Distributing workloads across multiple servers prevents any single server from being overwhelmed, thus reducing the risk of failure.

Reactive Recovery Strategies

Incident Response Plans: Setting up structured incident response protocols allows organizations to respond quickly and effectively to system failures. This includes defining roles, coordinating resources, and communicating with stakeholders.

Automated Rollbacks: In software systems, automated rollback mechanisms can revert applications to their last stable state in case of failure, minimizing downtime.

Post-Incident Reviews: After a failure, conducting a thorough review helps organizations learn from the incident and improve future response strategies and system design.

Case Study: Online Banking Systems

To illustrate graceful degradation and recovery strategies in practice, we can examine the case of online banking systems. These systems must maintain trust and reliability, as they deal with sensitive financial transactions.

Graceful Degradation in Online Banking

Suppose an online banking platform experiences a temporary outage of its real-time transaction processing system. Rather than rendering the entire platform unusable, the bank implements graceful degradation by allowing users to access their account balances, view recent transactions, and make fund transfers using stored information or batch processes. While real-time operations are not available, critical functionalities remain accessible, preserving user trust and satisfaction.

Recovery Strategies in Online Banking

In case of a system failure, the online banking platform's reactive approach could include:

Automated alerts to notify both users and IT teams of the incident so that responses can be initiatedswiftly.
A dedicated disaster recovery site that can take over in the event of a critical failure at the primarydata center.
Continuous backups of user transactions and data, enabling quick restoration once the system is backonline.

By designing systems with the ability to handle failures gracefully, organizations can enhance reliability, maintain user satisfaction, and minimize the impact of interruptions. As we advance into an era where systems become increasingly complex and interdependent, understanding these concepts will be crucial forengineers, stakeholders, and anyone involved in system design and management.

Chapter 12: Monitoring and Intrusion Detection

In this chapter, we will explore how to implement effective monitoring and intrusion detection systems usingGo. The Go programming language, known for its efficiency, simplicity, and powerful concurrency features, is particularly suited for building high-performance network applications, making it an excellent choice for developing these systems.

Understanding Monitoring and Intrusion Detection
What is Monitoring?
Monitoring involves the continuous observation of a system's performance and health. In the context of network security, monitoring helps in identifying unusual activities or anomalies that could indicate potential security breaches. Effective monitoring relies on the collection, analysis, and visualization of logs and metrics.

What is Intrusion Detection?

Intrusion Detection involves identifying unauthorized access or anomalies in a network or system. IDS can be divided into two main categories:

Network-Based Intrusion Detection Systems (NIDS) - Monitors network traffic for suspiciousactivity.

Host-Based Intrusion Detection Systems (HIDS) - Monitors individual devices for signs ofcompromise.

In this chapter, we will focus primarily on NIDS but will touch on aspects relevant to HIDS as well.## Setting Up a Basic Monitoring Framework in Go

Before diving into the specifics of intrusion detection, it is imperative to establish a monitoring framework.We will utilize Go's `net/http` package to build a simple server that collects log data, which can later be analyzed for anomalies.

Building a Simple HTTP Logger

Here is a simple example of an HTTP server that logs incoming requests:

```go
package main

import ( "log" "net/http""time"
)

func logRequest(r *http.Request) {
log.Printf("Received request: %s %s from %s at %s",
r.Method,          r.URL,          r.RemoteAddr,
time.Now().Format(time.RFC1123))

}

func handler(w http.ResponseWriter, r *http.Request) {
logRequest(r)
w.Write([]byte("Hello, World!"))
}

func main() { http.HandleFunc("/", handler)
```

```go
    log.Println("Starting server on :8080")
    if err := http.ListenAndServe(":8080", nil); err != nil {
        log.Fatalf("Error starting server: %v", err)
    }
}
```

This code sets up a basic web server that logs each incoming request with details such as the method, URL, IP address, and timestamp. In a real-world application, you would likely want to store this data in a more structured way, potentially in a database or a log management solution.

Implementing Intrusion Detection ### Anomaly Detection Using Patterns

One of the simplest ways to detect intrusions is to check incoming requests against known patterns or signatures of malicious behavior. For example, repeated failed login attempts or unusual request methods can indicate an attempted intrusion.

You can build a simple anomaly detection mechanism with a request rate limiter that tracks the number of requests per IP over a specified time window:

```go
package main

import ( "log" "net/http""sync"
"time"
)
```

```go
type RateLimiter struct { mu        sync.Mutex      requests
            map[string]int
requestTime map[string]time.Timelimitint
window       time.Duration
}

func NewRateLimiter(limit int, window time.Duration)
*RateLimiter {rl := &RateLimiter{
requests:           make(map[string]int), requestTime:
make(map[string]time.Time),limit:       limit,

window:      window,
}
go rl.cleanup()return rl
}

func (rl *RateLimiter) Allow(ip string) bool {rl.mu.Lock()
defer rl.mu.Unlock()

now := time.Now()
if  _,  found  :=  rl.requestTime[ip];  !found  {
rl.requestTime[ip] = now
}

if   now.Sub(rl.requestTime[ip])   >   rl.window   {
rl.requests[ip] = 1
rl.requestTime[ip] = nowreturn true
}

rl.requests[ip]++
if rl.requests[ip] > rl.limit {
return false // Rate limit exceeded
}
```

```go
    return true
}

var limiter = NewRateLimiter(5, 10*time.Second) // 5
requests every 10 seconds

func handler(w http.ResponseWriter, r *http.Request) { ip
:= r.RemoteAddr
if !limiter.Allow(ip) {
http.Error(w,        "Too        many        requests",
http.StatusTooManyRequests)   log.Printf("Rate    limit
exceeded for %s", ip)
return
}

log.Printf("Received request: %s %s from %s", r.Method,
r.URL, ip)w.Write([]byte("Hello, World!"))
}

// main function remains the same
```

In this implementation, the `RateLimiter` tracks the number of requests from each IP address and blocks excessive requests, logging the event appropriately. This is a straightforward method to detect potential scanning or brute-force attacks.

Enhanced Intrusion Detection with Machine Learning

For more sophisticated applications, you may wish to

incorporate machine learning algorithms to analyze patterns in your log data. Go has libraries like `gonum` and `golearn` which can help in building predictive models.

You can train a model on historical log data to identify patterns indicative of malicious behavior and then deploy the model in your monitoring system to flag potential intrusions in real-time.

Integrating with Existing Tools

While building a custom monitoring and intrusion detection system can be beneficial, it can also be helpful to integrate your solution with existing tools and frameworks that specialize in security. Tools like Elasticsearch, Logstash, and Kibana (the ELK stack) can be used to visualize log data, while systems like Suricata or Snort may offer additional signature-based detection capabilities.

To send logs to an ELK stack from your Go application, you can utilize the `github.com/olivere/elastic` package to interact with Elasticsearch:

```go
package main

// Include necessary importsimport (
"context" "github.com/olivere/elastic/v7"
)

// Initializing your logger to send logs here
```

```
func sendLogToElasticsearch(logMessage string) {client,
err := elastic.NewClient()
if err != nil {
log.Printf("Error creating ElasticSearch client: %v", err)
return
}

_, err = client.Index().
Index("logs").                      BodyJson(logMessage).
Do(context.Background())
if err != nil {
log.Printf("Error indexing document: %v", err)
}
}

// Adjust the logging to include a call to
`sendLogToElasticsearch`
```

This code demonstrates how to send logs directly to an Elasticsearch instance for centralized management and analysis.

Effective monitoring and intrusion detection are vital components of a comprehensive cybersecurity strategy. By leveraging Go's capabilities, you can build scalable, high-performance systems that not only notify you of potential threats but also analyze patterns for ongoing protection.

Setting Up Monitoring Tools for Your Go Applications

Go, known for its efficiency and performance in concurrent programming, is widely used in cloud services, microservices, and other modern architectures. This chapter will guide you through the process of setting up monitoring tools for your Go applications, helping you ensure their optimal operation.

Understanding the Importance of Monitoring

Monitoring involves gathering, analyzing, and acting on metrics related to your application's performance. Effective monitoring enables you to:

Detect issues early: With real-time visibility into your application's health, you can catch problems before they impact your users.
Understand usage patterns: By analyzing usage metrics, you can make informed decisions about features, scaling, and improvements.
Optimize performance: Identify bottlenecks and improve resource utilization.
Ensure reliability: Monitor key health indicators to reduce downtime and enhance service quality. ## Key Metrics to Monitor
Before we dive into setting up monitoring tools, it's essential to identify the key metrics you should track in your Go applications:

Application Performance Metrics:
Response time: Time taken to complete requests.

Throughput: Number of requests processed per second.

System Resource Metrics:
CPU usage: Percentage of CPU time consumed by your application.
Memory usage: Total memory consumption and garbage collection metrics.

Error Metrics:
Error rates: Frequency of application errors.
Latency: Time taken for error requests.

Custom Business Metrics:
User interactions: Track specific actions your users perform within the application.
Transaction volumes: Monitor the business value of transactions processed.## Choosing Monitoring Tools
There are numerous monitoring tools available, and the best choice for your Go application depends on your specific needs. Here are some popular tools that seamlessly integrate with Go:

1. Prometheus

Prometheus is an open-source monitoring and alerting toolkit that is particularly suitable for cloud-native applications. It operates based on a pull model, gathering metrics from configured endpoints at specified intervals.

Setting Up Prometheus:
Integrate Prometheus with Go: Use the `prometheus/client_golang` library to expose metrics.

```go
import (
"github.com/prometheus/client_golang/prometheus"
"github.com/prometheus/client_golang/prometheus/promhttp"
"net/http"
)

func main() {
http.Handle("/metrics", promhttp.Handler())
go func() {
for {
// Collect metrics and expose them via /metrics
}
}()
http.ListenAndServe(":8080", nil)
}
```

Configure the Prometheus server: Define the scrape configuration in `prometheus.yml`.

```yaml
scrape_configs:
job_name: 'go_app'
static_configs:
- targets: ['localhost:8080']
```

2. Grafana

Grafana is often used in conjunction with Prometheus, providing a powerful visualization layer for your metrics. You can set up dashboards to visualize everything from CPU usage to response times.

Setting Up Grafana:

Install Grafana and configure it to use Prometheus as a data source.
Create dashboards with panels that visualize the metrics collected by Prometheus.### 3. ELK Stack (Elasticsearch, Logstash, Kibana)
For logging and performance metrics, the ELK stack is widely used. It collects and analyzes log data, offering high-scale distributed logging.

Integrate Logrus or another logging library to structure your logs.
Use Logstash to collect and ship logs to Elasticsearch.
Visualize the logs and identify trends using Kibana.### 4. Datadog
Datadog is a cloud-based monitoring service that supports various programming languages, including Go. It provides agents that automatically collect metrics, logs, and request traces.

Setting Up Datadog:
Install the Datadog agent and configure it for your Go application.
Use the `datadog-go` library for custom metrics and traces.

5. New Relic

Similar to Datadog, New Relic provides full-stack observability with APM, infrastructure monitoring, and logging features.

Integrate the New Relic Go agent into your application for performance monitoring.

Use New Relic to track transaction traces and error analytics. ## Best Practices for Monitoring Go Applications
Instrument Your Code: Use libraries and frameworks that facilitate instrumentation for monitoring, such as Prometheus and OpenTelemetry.

Set Up Alerts: Configure alerts based on key metrics to ensure prompt responses to anomalies. For example, if CPU usage exceeds a defined threshold, trigger alerts to notify the DevOps team.

Contextual Logging: Ensure that your logs include sufficient context (e.g., request IDs) to correlate logs with performance metrics.

Evaluate Regularly: Regularly review metrics and alerts to refine what you track and improve system performance.

Use Distributed Tracing: For microservices-based architectures, consider setting up distributed tracing with tools like OpenTelemetry or Jaeger for tracking requests as they traverse services.

Setting up effective monitoring tools for your Go applications is foundational to maintaining application performance and reliability. By employing the right tools and best practices, you can ensure your applications remain healthy, performant, and responsive to user needs. In the next chapters, we will delve deeper into specific use cases, including handling error tracking and advanced monitoring techniques tailored for microservices architectures.

Detecting and Responding to Security Breaches

This chapter provides a comprehensive overview of strategies, tools, and best practices for detecting and responding to security breaches in Go environments.

Understanding Security Breaches

A security breach occurs when an unauthorized entity gains access to a system, application, or network, potentially leading to data theft, data manipulation, service disruptions, and other damaging impacts.
Breaches can result from various factors, including software vulnerabilities, human errors, and malicious attacks.

As Go applications are commonly used in backend services, API development, and cloud-native environments, it is especially essential to build robust processes for breach detection and response.

Detecting Security Breaches

Detecting security breaches in software applications requires a combination of preventive measures, monitoring tools, and logging mechanisms.

1. **Implementing Proper Logging**

Logging is crucial for maintaining an audit trail and

204

diagnosing issues post-breach. Go provides an efficient way to implement logging through its standard library. Developers should consider:

Structured Logging: Use libraries like `logrus` or `zap` for structured logging. This allows for easy parsing and querying in log management tools.
Log Level Management: Utilize log levels (info, warn, error, fatal) to differentiate the significance of log entries.
Data Sensitivity: Avoid logging sensitive information such as passwords and personally identifiable information (PII). Instead, measure and log events without compromising data security.

Example of structured logging in Go:

```go
package main

import ( "github.com/sirupsen/logrus"
)

func main() {
logger := logrus.New() logger.WithFields(logrus.Fields{
"event": "user_login","user": "johndoe",
}).Info("User login attempted")
}
```

2. **Monitoring and Alerting Systems**

Real-time monitoring of your Go applications can help spot anomalies indicative of a potential security breach.

Consider the following tools and techniques:

Prometheus & Grafana: Integrate Go applications with Prometheus to collect metrics and configure Grafana for visualization and monitoring. Set up alerts for unusual activity (e.g., a sudden increase in error rates).
Intrusion Detection Systems: Implement tools such as OSSEC or Snort to monitor system integrity and generate alerts based on suspicious activities.

3. **Anomaly Detection**

Advanced monitoring can incorporate machine learning techniques to recognize patterns and flag deviations. Libraries like `go-ml` can be utilized to implement anomaly detection algorithms.

4. **Security Scanning Tools**

Utilize static analysis tools to identify vulnerabilities in your Go codebase:

Gosec: A static analysis tool specifically designed for Go applications, which detects common security issues.
Golint: Helps enforce coding standards, which can indirectly prevent security flaws due to poor coding practices.

Responding to Security Breaches

Despite robust detection mechanisms, breaches will occur. Implementing a well-defined incident response plan is essential for minimizing the effects of a breach.

1. **Incident Response Plan**

An incident response plan should include:

Roles and Responsibilities: Define clear roles for team members involved in the response process, including communication, technical remediation, and documentation.
Breach Detection and Classification: Establish protocols for how to verify breaches and classify their severity for appropriate response measures.

2. **Containment Measures** Once a breach is detected:
Isolate Affected Systems: Remove compromised systems from the network to prevent the spread of the breach.
Change Credentials: Immediately alter access controls and credentials for affected systems to block unauthorized access.

3. **Analysis and Remediation**

Post-breach, conduct a thorough analysis to understand how the breach occurred and what vulnerabilities were exploited:

Root Cause Analysis (RCA): Identify underlying issues, whether they be coding flaws, configuration errors, or human mistakes.
Patching and Upgrades: Implement necessary patches to rectify identified vulnerabilities in your Go application.

4. **Communication Plan**

Communicate with stakeholders, including team members, affected users, and regulatory bodies where necessary:

Transparency: Provide affected users with clear and concise information about the breach, potential impacts, and recommended actions.
Post-Mortem Review: Conduct a post-incident review to evaluate the response effectiveness and learn lessons for future prevention.

5. **Regular Security Audits**

Finally, conduct regular audits of both your code and infrastructure to ensure compliance with security policies and to identify areas for improvement.

By implementing proactive measures, establishing robust monitoring and logging frameworks, and developing comprehensive incident response plans, developers can significantly mitigate the risks associated with security breaches.

Conclusion

In a world where digital threats are ever-evolving, ensuring the security of web applications is more essential than ever. Throughout this book, "Web Security with Go: Build Safe and Resilient Applications," we have explored the foundational principles of web security and how Go provides a robust framework for developing secure applications.

We began by examining the importance of security in the web landscape, highlighting common vulnerabilities and the devastating consequences they can have. Armed with this understanding, we delvedinto the specific tools and techniques within the Go ecosystem that enable developers to mitigate risks effectively.

From implementing secure authentication and authorization mechanisms to safeguarding data through encryption and secure coding practices, we provided actionable insights and practical examples to enhanceyour application's security posture. Furthermore, we emphasized the significance of staying updated with security trends and continuously monitoring your applications for vulnerabilities.

As you conclude your journey through this book, remember that web security is not just a one-time task but an ongoing commitment. The landscape of cybersecurity is constantly changing, and as a developer, your dedication to maintaining and improving your security practices will be crucial in safeguarding your applications and users.

We encourage you to implement what you've learned, conduct regular security audits, and foster a culture of security-aware development within your team. By doing so, you're not only enhancing the resilience of your applications but also contributing to a safer web environment for all.

Biography

Tommy Clark is a passionate and dynamic author who combines a deep love for technology with an insatiable curiosity for innovation. As the mastermind behind the book *"Clark: A Journey Through Expertise and Innovation,"* Tommy brings years of hands-on experience in web development, web applications, and system administration to the forefront, offering readers a unique and insightful perspective.

With a strong background in Go programming and an ever-evolving fascination with crafting robust, efficient systems, Tommy excels at turning complex technical concepts into practical, actionable strategies. Whether building cutting-edge web solutions or diving into the intricate details of system optimization, Tommy's expertise is both broad and profound.

When not immersed in coding or writing, Tommy enjoys exploring the latest tech trends, tinkering with open-source projects, and mentoring aspiring developers. His enthusiasm for technology and dedication to empowering others shine through in everything he creates.

Join Tommy Clark on this exciting journey to unlock the full potential of technology—and get ready to be inspired, informed, and equipped to tackle your next big challenge!

Glossary: Web Security with Go

A

Authentication
The process of verifying the identity of a user or system. In web applications, authentication ensures that users are who they claim to be, often through methods such as username/password combinations, OAuth tokens, or multi-factor authentication.

Authorization
The process of determining what an authenticated user is allowed to do. It involves defining user roles and permissions to control access to various resources and functionalities within an application.

B

Brute Force Attack
An attempt to gain unauthorized access to a system by systematically checking all possible passwords or keys until the correct one is found. This method is often employed against login forms.

C

Cross-Site Request Forgery (CSRF)
A security exploit where an attacker tricks a user into executing unwanted actions on a different web application in which the user is authenticated. Protecting against CSRF typically involves using anti-CSRF tokens.

Cross-Site Scripting (XSS)
A vulnerability that allows an attacker to inject malicious scripts into web pages viewed by other users. This script execution can lead to data theft, session hijacking, and other malicious activities.

D

Data Encryption
The method of converting sensitive information into an unreadable format to prevent unauthorized access. In Go, developers can use the `crypto` package to implement various encryption algorithms for securing data at rest and in transit.

I

Input Validation
The process of verifying that the data received from users meets expected criteria before processing it. This practice helps mitigate risks associated with injection attacks and ensures the integrity of the application data.

M

Multi-Factor Authentication (MFA)
An authentication method that requires two or more verification factors from independent categories of credentials, adding an extra layer of security beyond just a password.

O

Open Web Application Security Project (OWASP)
A non-profit organization focused on improving the security of software. OWASP provides a wealth of resources, including top ten lists of web vulnerabilities and best practices for web security.

R

Rate Limiting
A technique used to control the amount of incoming requests to a web application over a certain period. By implementing rate limiting, developers can protect their applications from abuse, such as denial-of-service attacks.

S

Secure Socket Layer (SSL)/Transport Layer Security (TLS)
Protocols used to establish a secure and encrypted connection between a client and a server. Go supports SSL/TLS through its `crypto/tls` package, enabling secure communication for web applications.

SQL Injection
A code injection technique that exploits vulnerabilities in an application's software by manipulating SQL queries. It occurs when user input is not properly sanitized, allowing attackers to execute arbitrary SQL code.

T

Token-Based Authentication
An authentication method in which a user receives a token

after logging in, which is then used for subsequent requests. This method is commonly used in RESTful APIs to authenticate users and maintain sessions without storing session data on the server.

X

XML External Entity (XXE)
A security vulnerability that arises when an XML parser processes external entities, allowing attackers to gain access to sensitive data or execute attacks on the server. Properly configuring XML parsers can helpmitigate this risk.

www.ingramcontent.com/pod-product-compliance
Lightning Source LLC
LaVergne TN
LVHW022342060326
832902LV00022B/4186